access to

is to be retu

D0346804

BRITAIN: ECONOMY, SOCIETY *and* INDUSTRIAL RELATIONS 1900–39

Second Edition

Robert Pearce

ughton

A MEMBER OF THE HODDER HEADLINE GROUP

Acknowledgements

The front cover illustration is a portrait of Ernest Bevin by Thomas Cantrell Dugdale, 1945, reproduced courtesy of National Portrait Gallery, London.

The publishers would like to thank the following individuals, institutions and companies for permission to reproduce copyright illustrations in this book: Communist Party Library, Picture Library and Archive, London, pages 97 and 98; David Low/Atlantic/original in the possession of Dr W.M. Keynes, page 126; Punch, pages 46 and 103.

The publishers would also like to thank the following for permission to reproduce material in this book: extracts from *The Road to Wigan Pier* by George Orwell (Copyright © George Orwell, 1936), by permission of Bill Hamilton as the Literary Executor of the Estate of the Late Sonia Brownell Orwell and Martin Secker & Warburg Ltd; Blackwell Publishers Ltd for the extracts from *They Saw It Happen 1897–1940* by Asa Briggs, Blackwell & Mott, 1960; extract from *English Journey* by J.B. Priestly published by Heinemann. Used by permission of The Random House Group Limited; Routledge for the extract from *The Gold Standard and Employment Policies between the Wars* by Sidney Pollard, Methuen, 1970; Sutton Publishing Limited for the extract from *British Trade Unionism, c.1770–1990* by Keith Laybourn, Sutton Publishing Ltd.

Every effort has been made to trace and acknowledge ownership of copyright. The publishers will be glad to make suitable arrangements with any copyright holders whom it has not been possible to contact.

Orders: please contact Bookpoint Ltd, 130 Milton Park, Abingdon, Oxon OX14 4SB. Telephone: (44) 01235 827720. Fax: (44) 01235 400454. Lines are open from 9.00 – 6.00, Monday to Saturday, with a 24 hour message answering service.

British Library Cataloguing in Publication Data
A catalogue record for this title is available from the British Library

ISBN 0 340 845813

First Published 2002
Impression number   10 9 8 7 6 5 4 3 2 1
Year   2008 2007 2006 2005 2004 2003 2002

Copyright © 2002 Robert Pearce

Typeset by Fakenham Photosetting, Fakenham, Norfolk.
Printed in Great Britain for Hodder & Stoughton Educational, a division of Hodder Headline Plc, 338 Euston Road, London NW1 3BH by Bath Press.

Contents

Preface

To the general reader

Although the *Access to History* series has been designed with the needs of students studying the subject at higher examination levels very much in mind, it also has a great deal to offer the general reader. The main body of the text (i.e. ignoring the 'Study Guides' at the ends of chapters) forms a readable and yet stimulating survey of a coherent topic as studied by historians. However, each author's aim has not merely been to provide a clear explanation of what happened in the past (to interest and inform): it has also been assumed that most readers wish to be stimulated into thinking further about the topic and to form opinions of their own about the significance of the events that are described and discussed (to be challenged). Thus, although no prior knowledge of the topic is expected on the reader's part, she or he is treated as an intelligent and thinking person throughout. The author tends to share ideas and possibilities with the reader, rather than passing on numbers of so-called 'historical truths'.

To the student reader

Although advantage has been taken of the publication of a second edition to ensure the results of recent research are reflected in the text, the main alteration from the first edition is the inclusion of new features, and the modification of existing ones, aimed at assisting you in your study of the topic at AS level, A level and Higher. Two features are designed to assist you during your first reading of a chapter. The *Points to Consider* section following each chapter title is intended to focus your attention on the main theme(s) of the chapter, and the issues box following most section headings alerts you to the question or questions to be dealt with in the section. The *Working on...* section at the end of each chapter suggests ways of gaining maximum benefit from the chapter.

There are many ways in which the series can be used by students studying History at a higher level. It will, therefore, be worthwhile thinking about your own study strategy before you start your work on this book. Obviously, your strategy will vary depending on the aim you have in mind, and the time for study that is available to you.

If, for example, you want to acquire a general overview of the topic in the shortest possible time, the following approach will probably be the most effective:

1. Read chapter 1. As you do so, keep in mind the issues raised in the *Points to Consider* section.
2. Read the *Points to Consider* section at the beginning of chapter 2 and decide whether it is necessary for you to read this chapter.

3. If it is, read the chapter, stopping at each heading or sub-heading to note down the main points that have been made. Often, the best way of doing this is to answer the question(s) posed in the Key Issues boxes.
4. Repeat stage 2 (and stage 3 where appropriate) for all the other chapters.

If, however, your aim is to gain a thorough grasp of the topic, taking however much time is necessary to do so, you may benefit from carrying out the same procedure with each chapter, as follows:

1. Try to read the chapter in one sitting. As you do this, bear in mind any advice given in the *Points to Consider* section.
2. Study the flow diagram at the end of the chapter, ensuring that you understand the general 'shape' of what you have just read.
3. Read the *Working on...* section and decide what further work you need to do on the chapter. In particularly important sections of the book, this is likely to involve reading the chapter a second time and stopping at each heading and sub-heading to think about (and probably to write a summary of) what you have just read.
4. Attempt the *Source-based questions* section. It will sometimes be sufficient to think through your answers, but additional understanding will often be gained by forcing yourself to write them down.

When you have finished the main chapters of the book, study the 'Further Reading' section and decide what additional reading (if any) you will do on the topic.

This book has been designed to help make your studies both enjoyable and successful. If you can think of ways in which this could have been done more effectively, please contact us. In the meantime, we hope that you will gain greatly from your study of History.

Keith Randell & Robert Pearce

Introduction

POINTS TO CONSIDER

The first part of this chapter deals with important developments during the period before 1900. Only if you grasp these changes in Britain's economy and society can you see the period 1900–39 in perspective. The second part introduces you to issues which will be treated at greater length in subsequent chapters. Your aim should be to grasp the main points – and thus acquire a 'mental map' of the rest of the book, rather than learn detailed factual information.

Those who have never studied British history from 1900 to 1939 may nevertheless be inclined to think that they understand this period. So strong are 'folk memories' from the past that almost everyone, from the field of social history, is aware of the so-called 'Edwardian idyll', a glorious, secure and somehow innocent period when, according to one of George Orwell's characters, it was 'somehow summer all year round' – and an era that ended abruptly with the carnage on the Western Front in the 1914–18 war. Many believe that Britain never recovered from the war and that its 'golden age' was henceforth behind it. From industrial history, we have all heard of the General Strike of 1926, when almost the entire population took sides in the most spectacular industrial dispute in British history. Industrial relations are popularly supposed, on the basis of this event, to have amounted to little more than bitter and sterile confrontation. Similarly British economic performance over the same period is generally seen as a process of dismal decline. No particular event stands out: instead, a whole decade is remembered. The 1930s are enshrined in the popular consciousness as 'a low, dishonest decade', 'the devil's decade', powerfully symbolised by the dole queue and the hunger marches. The Thirties are seen as both the worst decade of the period and yet, at the same time, as in some way typical of a much longer time-span.

Readers, at this stage, may be excused for supposing that this is going to be a pessimistic and rather depressing book! But in fact these 'folk memories' are very limited, one-sided interpretations of the past, demonstrating the truth of the oft-quoted assertion that 'a little learning is a dangerous thing'. Indeed popular images of the past often hinder true understanding. Such myths are difficult to dispel, but as historians we must try to put aside preconceptions and penetrate to the reality of the past – which is always more varied and interesting than any simple, single image. But before we look at 1900–1939 we must review the nineteenth century. For just as we cannot understand the present without knowing the past, so we cannot understand any period of the past without understanding *its* historical background.

1 Nineteenth-century Economy and Society

> **KEY ISSUES** What were the main economic changes that occurred and how did these affect the structure of British society?

a) The Economy

In the middle of the nineteenth century Britain was the world's strongest economic power. Already, from about 1760, the country had undergone substantial economic growth: the power of the water-wheel had been harnessed to drive cotton-spinning machinery, with a resulting massive increase in the output of the textile industry. Then, in the first half of the nineteenth century, the steam engine had been used to supply an even greater motive power to machines. As a result, Britain became the 'workshop of the world'. Many historians have criticised the term 'industrial revolution' to describe this process because it seems to imply a more rapid and complete economic change than in fact occurred, especially since much of Britain remained relatively immune to the growth of industry and saw more continuity than change. Nevertheless, it remains true that large parts of Britain were dramatically transformed by industrialisation, as was the country's place in the world economy.

In the middle of the nineteenth century Britain produced two-thirds of the world's coal, half the world's iron, five-sevenths of its steel, and half its cotton goods. Britain was exporting far more than any other nation, and was also importing more food and raw materials than any other. A country with only two per cent of the world's population was producing a staggering 40 per cent of the world's manufactured goods. Britain's economic strength lay primarily in its so-called 'staple industries' – textiles, coal, iron and steel, and shipbuilding – while the financial, banking and insurance services offered by the City of London further added to the strength and profitability of the economy.

The supposed causes of this economic success did not long escape the penetrating eye of the Victorians. It appeared obvious that it was due to their inventiveness, skill and capacity for hard work; in short, to their all-round superiority. Clouded by their own conceit, many Victorians decided that they must be God's new chosen people. ('Being an Englishman,' noted Cecil Rhodes, 'is the greatest prize in the lottery of life.') Historians, however, have seen it rather differently. Most have argued that industrialisation was caused by a complex combination of factors (including population growth, the availability of capital, and technological inventions) simply coming together in Britain first. Britain's industrial supremacy over other countries in the mid-nineteenth century was, in the words of one historian, largely a 'happy accident'. Britain was the world's first industrial nation, and it achieved a substantial lead not because it was 'better' than other countries but simply because it began the race before potential competitors were even at the starting line.

b) Society

This economic growth affected the way of life of most of Britain's population. A basically agrarian society gave way to an industrial one. In 1851, for the first time, just over 50 per cent of the population of England and Wales lived in urban rather than rural areas, and by 1901 over 75 per cent lived in towns. The total population also increased dramatically, growing by over 80 per cent in the half-century up to 1901.

The most characteristic form of employment became factory labour, and as the century proceeded a growing sense of 'class identity' occurred. At the start of the century most 'workers' had no consciousness of being part of the same group, but by about 1900 a greater – though far from total – cohesion was beginning to appear. The British population was made up of a small landed aristocracy (the traditional rulers of agrarian society), the middle classes (the owners and managers of the factories, as well as the traders and professionals) and, the largest group of all (comprising around three-quarters of the total population), the working classes – the plural being preferred to the singular because of the wide variations in pay that existed amongst wage-earners. Some skilled workers could earn a very good living, but for most unskilled workers – who might have to work for 15 hours at a stretch during 'brisk' times – wages were often appallingly low. On average 'real wages' (that is, wages in relation to prices, or 'purchasing power') per head of the population in Britain quadrupled during the nineteenth century, but not everyone shared equally in this growing prosperity. Far from it. Britain's towns and cities saw a high degree of social segregation, with the rich enjoying better housing, better food, wider educational and cultural opportunities, as well as being healthier and living longer.

Social investigators like Seebohm Rowntree established at the start of the twentieth century that around a third of Britons lived in poverty, especially since the wages of an unskilled labourer were insufficient to keep a family 'in a state of bare physical efficiency'. Many workers complained of gross exploitation by their employers. Some thought that a violent revolution would be necessary to end this state of affairs, but far more turned for help to trade unions in order to secure improvements within existing capitalist society.

2 Nineteenth-century Trade Unionism

> **KEY ISSUES** Why did the trade unions grow in this period? How did their character change?

Trade unionism achieved substantial success during the nineteenth century. Yet no one in 1800 could have predicted the growth that was to occur. Indeed in this year unions were illegal, such 'combinations' being associated with the revolutionary ideas current across the Channel in the homeland of Britain's enemy, France. Although the legal ban was removed in 1824, the nature of legitimate trade union activity – of what, in law, unions should be allowed to do – was still a matter for controversy. Yet whatever the legal position, many employers simply refused to recognise the existence of trade unions amongst their employees and would not bargain with them. Partly as a result of this, trade unions were slow to develop and did so in piecemeal fashion. Only in the 1850s did they make significant progress.

In 1851 the Amalgamated Society of Engineers (ASE) was founded, with engineers throughout the country coming together to press for improvements in their industry. It turned out to be only the first of a group referred to by historians as the 'new model unions'. The ASE and its imitators were 'craft' unions, combinations of highly skilled and well-paid men, sometimes dubbed the 'labour aristocracy'. They were exclusive organisations, only open to particular workers, their aims being to maintain or increase their wage levels, to improve their conditions of work and also to ensure that only men with the requisite levels of skill could enter their particular trade. Membership fees were usually high, providing not only for the employment of full-time union officials but for sick pay, funeral expenses and other benefits. Members of these unions did not believe in general working-class solidarity, and although a few unions for less skilled workers did exist in this period the great bulk of unskilled and semi-skilled men and women did not belong to any union.

During 1850–75 the economy expanded rapidly and trade unionism made significant advances. Membership rose from about 100,000 in 1850 to more than one million in 1875. In 1869 the Trades Union Congress (TUC) was formed to give a collective voice to the craft unions. Nevertheless, the main weakness of the movement was still the small numbers of unskilled and semi-skilled members, and the period after 1875 seemed to provide difficult conditions for further expansion. Membership declined substantially as the economy contracted.

Even so, important developments took place from the late 1880s. In 1888 several union leaders called for the unionisation of all workers, and over the next few years the 'new unions' emerged. These organisations differed from the old craft unions: they admitted unskilled and semi-skilled workers and were 'general' unions, embracing all workers in a particular industry and not just those men and women performing the same functions. Almost immediately they proved their power, winning two well-publicised strikes – the match girls' strike in 1888 and the London dock strike the following year. After this boost to workers' aspirations union growth proceeded apace, and even white-collar workers formed their own organisations. In 1900 there were about two million trade union members, and the movement was much stronger than ever before. Yet trade unionism still had noticeable points of weakness. Most trade unionists were still skilled or semi-skilled men, so that the great majority of male workers – who were unskilled – did not belong to a union. In addition, only three per cent of women workers were trade unionists. In total, no more than about 15 per cent of all workers were unionised, and still only a minority of employers would recognise and negotiate with them. Furthermore, politicians had yet to make up their minds whether to treat the unions as friend or foe.

3 The Role of Governments

> **KEY ISSUES** What were the characteristic attitudes of governments on economic, industrial and social issues?

a) Official Attitudes to Trade Unions

Governments tended to be uncertain how to react to trade unions and, as a result, their position in law was not clearly defined. In 1824 Parliament gave unions legal recognition but failed to specify what they could and could not do. Once it became clear that the unions would not confine themselves to peaceful wage bargaining but would organise strikes, severe laws were passed against intimidation and obstruction during disputes. Hence, while government – through the law – was prepared to allow unions to exist, it was not prepared to allow them to mount effective strike action.

The 1870s saw several changes in the law. Legal protection was given to trade union funds, so that officials who stole members' money could be punished, and, most important of all, 'peaceful picketing' was allowed for the first time. Whereas, a few years earlier, men and women had been arrested merely for shouting insults at those who worked during a strike, now only acts of physical violence were punishable by law. Politicians seemed prepared to tolerate, though not encourage, the trade unions.

Political recognition of the unions was grudging, and as a result key issues were left undefined. Were unions immune to prosecution from employers whose profits had declined because of 'industrial action' (really industrial *in*action)? Equally important, in what sense, if any, did unions have the right to involve themselves in politics? Could trade unions sponsor candidates at elections, and pay their salaries if they were elected to Parliament? The first trade union representative entered the House of Commons in 1874, duly elected by his constituents, but to some this seemed a dangerous portent of union power. By the end of the nineteenth century politicians had still not fully come to terms with trade unionism.

b) Official Attitudes to Society and the Economy

Britain's spectacular industrial growth had not occurred as a result of government initiatives, and politicians therefore decided that they ought as far as possible to stand aside from economic affairs, pursuing a policy of *laissez-faire* (non-interventionism). But they could not totally detach themselves. They felt that they had to take action in some matters.

First, in the area of social policy, politicians came to accept as the nineteenth century wore on that they had to do something about working conditions, for instance by specifying the maximum number of hours women and children could work. They also had to take a hand in education (so that, with Acts in 1870 and 1880, state elementary education became compulsory). An expanding economy needed a workforce educated to certain levels, and at the same time state-sponsored education could foster values of patriotism, hard work and respectability among schoolchildren. In addition, governments had to take action to reduce the incidence of disease in Britain's cities and to provide some sort of relief for the 'deserving poor'.

Secondly, governments were concerned with 'finance', raising taxation to cover the costs of administration, social policy and defence. But they were determined not to hamstring industry by taxing it too heavily. The defence budget was therefore kept low, and governments were concerned to avoid wars. Peace was seen to be in the national interest. On the whole, it was generally believed that the less government, the better. Governments had to intervene occasionally, but in this period they did so with reluctance. If they stood aside from the economy as much as possible, allowing individuals to pursue their own self-interest, the maximum degree of economic prosperity would be sure to result – this was nineteenth-century economic wisdom.

4 Twentieth-century Themes

> **KEY ISSUES** What are the key issues of the 1900–39 period?

History is so vast that we can never hope to study more than a fraction of it. This is especially true for the twentieth century, about which so much evidence survives. So which elements should we select for particular scrutiny? Some themes seem to select themselves because they were so important in the past, while others are often chosen because they seem relevant and topical today. Those who look into the past often see a reflection of the issues and priorities current in their own times. Perhaps this is inevitable, but we should be on our guard lest present concerns lead us to distort the past by giving undue prominence to some aspects of it.

a) Trade Union Issues

Historians of the period 1900–39 have focused on several issues relating to trade unions. First, the theme of trade unionism in British law. This was an especially controversial issue in the period 1900–14. Initially unions were declared liable for damages sustained during strikes, and then they were declared immune. Similarly trade unionists were forbidden and then authorised to make contributions – by way of a 'political levy' – to a political party. In short, these were years of conflict and strife, all the more so because a sequence of extensive and sometimes violent strikes took place.

The war years, 1914–18, witnessed a lessening of strike activity and an increase of national solidarity in the face of the common enemy. Yet most historians have chosen instead to focus on the General Strike of 1926. This is possibly the most important single event of the interwar years, and it has aroused considerable debate. Three issues must be considered in some depth: the causes of the strike, the course of the nine-day conflict and why it lasted so short a time, and the consequences of the strike, including the 1927 Trade Disputes Act which re-opened the contentious issue of the position of the unions in law. It should be remembered, however, that other developments took place between the wars. In particular the trade union movement, under the direction of men such as Ernest Bevin (see the Profile on page 88), made a substantial recovery by the late-1930s, moving closer to the Labour Party and taking a greater interest in political affairs than ever before.

b) Economic Issues

The most common economic theme that has been identified in the period from 1900 to 1939 is that of Britain's economic decline. Perhaps historians have been obsessed with it and have, as a result, exaggerated its importance. Certainly it seems to have led some historians to neglect areas of the economy that were prospering. This emphasis on the nation's decline may stem partly from the fact that in the period after 1960 British people became acutely conscious that their country was falling behind its main rivals and therefore wished to trace the historical roots of this phenomenon.

Nevertheless it is understandable that this theme has been identified. After all, while in 1850 Britain had scarcely any economic rivals, at the start of the war in 1914 the United States and, in some respects, Germany were producing more than Britain. How important was the 1900–14 period in this process? Was the First World War an economic catastrophe for Britain? Most controversial of all is British economic performance in the interwar period, which has been attacked by some writers while being applauded by others. The economy in the 1920s has tended to be ignored, with historians focusing on the 'Great Depression' of 1929–33 and on the nature of the recovery that followed. No consensus on economic performance has emerged. Much has been written on the mass unemployment and poverty that existed, and indeed the 'Hungry Thirties' is the most common image people today have of this period. But 'revisionist' historians have insisted that the 1930s saw boom, with millions of jobs being created and affluence dawning. The period was essentially one of contrasts, marked by high regional unemployment – especially among those who had worked in the once prosperous 'staple' industries – but also by high productivity and by the creation of new industries.

A common delusion is that economic history is simply a matter of establishing statistics for output, prices and wages and so on – that it is essentially quantitative. As a result, it is sometimes thought that there is little scope for controversy or doubt or imagination – or indeed for interest! But such a view is entirely mistaken. Statistics are indeed important for economic history: they help us to express things with conciseness, and they can be vivid and even shocking. But they are not the be-all and end-all. Disraeli once said that there are three kinds of lies: 'lies, damned lies and [worst of all] statistics'. All too often statistics can be manipulated to prove whatever we want them to, and certainly they must be treated with extreme care. We really need to know how statistics were computed in the first place, how reliable they are and, above all, exactly what they tell us. Often economic history is highly controversial and its study involves the full range of historical skills – a calculator is useful, but critical intelligence is of far more value.

Another important economic theme from 1900 to 1939 is the growing involvement of governments in the economy. By the latter date politicians intervened far more in economic issues and *laissez-faire* was no longer their basic attitude. Indeed by the end of the interwar period politicians were being influenced by the interventionist views of the man who, in earlier days, had been the most outspoken critic of the financial establishment, John Maynard Keynes (see the Profile on page 123). Nevertheless it is important to realise that government involvement in the economy did not grow steadily. The years of war and its aftermath (1914–20) saw far greater government direction of the economy than at any other period covered by this book.

Did government intervention in the economy prove constructive and effective? Particularly important is the issue of how constructively politicians reacted to the Great Depression and whether more could have been done to provide work for the unemployed in the 1930s. Far from being an arid, purely 'factual' topic, this is a lively one which almost automatically reflects contemporary political views about the appropriate role of governments in economic life.

c) Social Issues

Social history is an endlessly fascinating subject. It is also one of the broadest, and hence we have to narrow our perspective and ask particular questions, prompted by the evidence that survives from the 1900–39 period and our own perspectives on it. These will include the following:

- What jobs did people pursue during these years?
- How did the Great War affect British society?
- How did the standard of living change?
- How did relations between the classes alter?
- What of relations between the sexes? Did the position of women in British society shift fundamentally?
- How did leisure activities (play rather than work) change?
- How did governments' activities – especially social legislation – affect British society?

It will be immediately apparent that social history is influenced by the work people do and the money they earn, and that therefore it is inseparable from economic history. Similarly it is affected by what politicians do. In an age of mass democracy – with important extensions of the franchise in 1918 and 1928 – politicians had to appeal to the electorate and, in a sense, 'buy' their votes. Hence there is no such thing as 'pure' social history, any more than there can be 'solely' economic history or 'unadulterated' political history. The different strands of history are part of a whole, each interacting with the others to form the complexity of the human past.

There are two further questions to consider:

- Did the lives of British people get better or worse between 1900 and 1939?
- How united was British society in 1900–39?

As we shall see, the attempt to grapple with these two wide-ranging issues involves all aspects of history, as well as all the abilities the historian can muster.

Summary Diagram

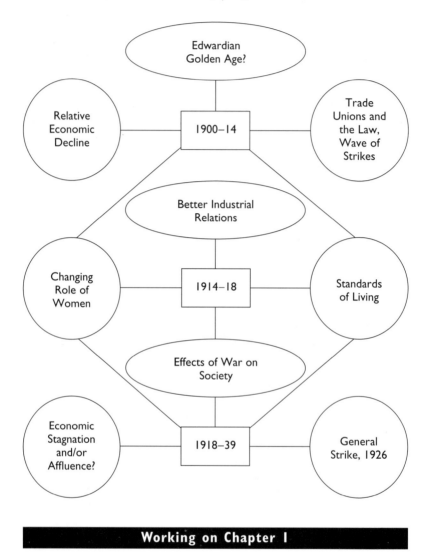

```
                    Edwardian
                    Golden Age?


   Relative                                    Trade
   Economic              1900–14           Unions and
   Decline                                   the Law,
                                            Wave of
                                             Strikes


                    Better Industrial
                       Relations


   Changing                                   Standards
   Role of              1914–18             of Living
   Women


                     Effects of War on
                         Society


   Economic                                    General
   Stagnation            1918–39           Strike, 1926
   and/or
   Affluence?
```

Working on Chapter 1

Detailed notes are not required. Instead, make sure that you understand the main issues and themes. You may find it worthwhile to refer back to this chapter, or at least to the study-diagram, to see how subsequent chapters form part of the book as a whole.

2 1900–14: Edwardian Idyll or Gathering Storm?

POINTS TO CONSIDER

This chapter provides an introduction to key features of Britain in 1900–14 – to the performance of the economy, to extremes of rich and poor in society, and to industrial relations. You will find it relatively easy to acquire factual information. But do not be satisfied simply with the 'facts'. Instead, you have to assess their significance. In particular, you have to grapple with two broad theories: that Edwardian Britain was a sort of 'golden age', cut tragically short by the outbreak of war in 1914; or, on the contrary, that social tensions, a rash of strikes and mounting economic problems render this a period foredoomed to failure.

KEY DATES

1900 Labour Representation Committee set up; two million trade union members.
1901 Rowntree's study of poverty in York published.
1902 Taff Vale case: unions liable for damages.
1906 Trade Disputes Act, reversing Taff Vale.
1907 Osborne Judgement, against financial support from the trade unions to the Labour Party.
1908 Old Age Pensions Act.
1910 Miners' strikes: one man killed in Tonypandy, two in Llanelli.
1911 11 million working days lost in strikes; Dockers' strike: 3 killed; National rail strike; Payment for MPs; National Insurance Act.
1912 41 million working days lost in strikes; national miners' strike, followed by Coal Mines Act.
1913 Trade Union Act, reversing Osborne Judgement: trade unions could impose a 'political levy'; transport strike in Dublin: 2 killed.
1914 4 million trade union members; (April) 'triple alliance' of miners, railwaymen and transport workers; (August) outbreak of First World War.

1 The British Economy in 1900

> **KEY ISSUE** What were the strengths and weaknesses of the British economy around 1900?

At the start of the twentieth century, Britain's economy was the most highly industrialised in the world. Its population, comprising only about two per cent of the world's total, was responsible for almost one-third of all trade in manufactured goods. Only the United States of America produced more goods than Britain, but per capita (that is, per head of population) Britain manufactured over 30 per cent more than the USA. In addition, Britain possessed the world's largest naval and merchant fleets, as well as the most extensive empire in history, covering about one-quarter of the world's land surface. This country invested far more capital abroad than any other, its currency (the pound sterling) was stronger than any other, and the City of London was the world's financial centre, acting as banker, money-lender and insurance broker on a vast scale.

The economy was strong and prosperous in 1900, remarkably so in view of Britain's tiny population and limited range of raw materials. Yet, although from our modern-day perspective we may be amazed at this economic success, there were many at the time who were dismayed at economic failure. They compared the position with the unrivalled supremacy enjoyed in the middle of the nineteenth century (see page 2). After all, only 20 years earlier Britain had been producing much more than the United States. Now, not only the USA but also Germany had overtaken British production of iron and steel.

British output was still increasing, but economic rivals were catching and even overtaking Britain. Many people became aware around 1900 that their country was experiencing an economic decline relative to its major competitors. Just before the start of the century a best-selling book, *Made in Germany*, had highlighted the degree to which German exports were penetrating the British market. Another volume, *American Invaders*, raised a similar warning about the United States. Now the difficulties Britain experienced in winning the Boer War (1899–1902) against Dutch settlers in South Africa seemed to underline British weakness. In Kipling's words, the British were given 'no end of a lesson'. It was popularly thought around this time (due to 'Social Darwinist' ideas) that unless a country was growing stronger, it would inevitably become weaker and decline. Was Britain therefore destined to follow the example of the Roman Empire – to decline and fall?

2 Edwardian Society

> **KEY ISSUES** Why have some described this period as Britain's 'golden age'? To what extent did poverty exist, and what was done to combat it?

a) Rich and Poor

In 1900–14 – a period often dubbed 'Edwardian' even though Edward VII was succeeded by George V in 1910 – many had no fears regarding continuing British prosperity. To them, it was the best of all possible worlds, and there seemed no reason why their idyllic existence should ever end. It was a period of 'conspicuous consumption' (a term newly coined) for the upper classes, of elegance and pleasure. Edwardian morality was much laxer than Victorian, Edward ('the Caresser') being a very different figure from his mother.

In her memoirs Marchioness Curzon of Kedleston recalled the period:

1 We went to our first Garden Party in the grounds of Windsor Castle ... The ladies of that time dressed beautifully in flowing summer dresses with flower-trimmed hats and lacy parasols ... We always had a large party for Ascot Races, and there were dinner parties and balls every
5 night during Race Week. These full days of gaiety involved frequent rapid changes of dress. We wore chiffon and lace dresses at Ascot, with large and becoming picture hats. We would rush home from the race-course and change quickly into linen or cotton dresses in order to go on the river, enjoying the late sunlight on the cushions of punts, or
10 sculling-boats, or small steam-launches, until it was time to change for dinner ... Every house was full and there was a vast amount of entertaining, in an agreeable, leisurely manner that few people now remember ... We enjoyed ourselves light-heartedly, and loved every minute of our lives. In retrospect, the summers seem to have been real summers
15 then – the river always sparkling in the sunlight, the sky always blue. When I write now of those light-hearted and enjoyable times it all sounds frivolous and trifling – but we were young then, and the shadows of this century had not yet fallen across our lives.

Many similar accounts of Edwardian Britain could be quoted. Yet most of them are from autobiographies written after the First World War (Lady Curzon's being published in 1955), and many people see their youth through rose-tinted spectacles. Indeed, after the horrors of the 'Great War', the pre-war years must have seemed like Paradise Lost. Furthermore, those who live privileged existences – made possible by droves of servants – often cultivate the habit of averting their eyes from sordid reality. Yet according to *The Times* of 19 January 1909, the majority of Britons had no illusions: 'They place the golden age behind them, and assume that no generation ever had to deal with evils so great and perplexing as those of the present day.'

One of the major problems of the time was the poverty of an uncomfortably large minority of the British population. According to the 1901 census there were 41.5 million people in the United Kingdom (a figure that had increased to over 45 million with the next decade). Three-quarters of these were working-class. Skilled workers could earn about £2 a week, but the average wage for the unskilled was around £1 a week. There were around 2 million unskilled workers, and so, with their dependants, there were something like 8 million people in Britain existing on this low wage. Labourers tended to have the largest families, their work was sometimes seasonal and they were liable to be the first to be laid off when trade was slack. Charles Booth had estimated that over 30 per cent of the population of London lived in poverty at the end of the nineteenth century. Now, in 1901, Seebohm Rowntree published the findings of research he had undertaken in 1899, showing that a similar number were afflicted in York. He argued that 10 per cent lived in 'primary poverty', earning insufficient to maintain health, while another 18 per cent were in 'secondary poverty' because they were not spending their income wisely. Clearly the health of those afflicted in this way was adversely affected, and during the Boer War of 1899–1902 40 per cent of recruits were rejected as physically unfit, a figure that reached 60 per cent in industrial cities like Leeds and Sheffield.

A flavour of working-class life before the First World War is provided in the memories of Robert Roberts, born in Salford in 1905:

1 Women wore their lives away washing clothes in heavy, iron-hooped tubs, scrubbing wood and stone, polishing furniture and fire-irons. There were housewives who finally lost real interest in anything save dirt removing ... The tragedy was that in the most opulent country in
5 the world so many possessed so little ... In general, slum life was far from being the jolly hive of communal activity that some romantics have claimed. They forget, perhaps, or never knew of the dirt that hung over all, of the rubbish that lay for months in the back alleys, of the 'entries' or ginnels with open middens where starving cats and dogs roamed or
10 died and lay for weeks unmoved. They did not know those houses that stank so badly through an open doorway that one stepped off the pavement to pass them by. That people stayed scrupulously clean in such surroundings – and many did – only proves the tenacity of the human spirit ... By 1912 the workhouses of England held some 280,000 pau-
15 pers: an all-time record.

Clearly life in Edwardian Britain was marked by extremes of poverty and riches. Indeed according to the historian Jose Harris, society at this time was 'more unequal than at any other period in national history'.

b) Government Legislation

Governments in the early twentieth century intervened far more decisively than their Victorian predecessors had done in an attempt to raise standards and alleviate poverty. There were several motives for their actions: the need to raise 'national efficiency' so that Britain could compete effectively against its rivals, the wish to prevent support for ('dish') the socialists, humanitarian concern, and the new interventionist philosophy of the 'New Liberals'. The most significant Acts were:

- The Education (Provision of Meals) Act of 1906, which allowed local authorities to provide school meals for needy children
- The Education (Administrative Provisions) Act of 1907, authorising medical inspection and treatment in schools
- The Children Act of 1908, establishing safeguards for neglected and abused children
- The Old Age Pensions Act of 1908, which provided a non-contributory pension of 5 shillings (25p) for those whose income was less than 7 shillings (40p) a week at the age of 70
- The National Insurance Act of 1911, which inaugurated a compulsory insurance scheme, providing treatment by a doctor, for all workers earning less than £160 a year. In addition, unemployment insurance was made compulsory for over 2 million workers whose trades were prone to unemployment.

Rowntree and others had established that there were particular points in the 'life-cycle' (e.g. in childhood, during bouts of ill health and unemployment, and in old age) when poverty was particularly likely to strike. The new Liberal legislation was designed to provide help at these times. Certainly it achieved some success. By 1914 around 14 million free schools meals were being provided per annum, there were nearly 1 million state pensioners, and around 14 million workers qualified for medical treatment and sick pay. Yet the benefits were low – at 5 shillings, an old age pension was only about a quarter of a labourer's wage – and, in the case of national insurance, were available only for strictly limited periods (26 weeks for sickness and 15 weeks for unemployment benefit). It was the industrial battle for a living wage, as we see below, which kept millions out of poverty.

3 Economic Trends, 1900–14

> **KEY ISSUES** What is meant by Britain's 'relative economic decline'? What were its causes?

a) The Views of Contemporaries

Many pessimistic commentators judged that Britain continued to decline after 1900. Germany was identified as the major threat. With its larger population (65 million compared with 45 million) and more abundant raw materials, Germany undoubtedly performed better economically, achieving a higher rate of growth. By 1913 it was responsible for a slightly higher percentage of world manufacturing output than Britain.

Yet if the fears of the pessimists seemed to be confirmed between 1900 and 1914, others were able to conclude that Britain was doing well and that the country had never been so prosperous. Britain's output was increasing. Many took comfort from this fact and mocked those who harked back nostalgically to the 'good old days' of unrivalled British supremacy. For example, while 100 million tons of coal had been mined in 1870, when Britain stood supreme, output rose to 287 million tons in 1913, a greater total than in any previous year. Progress was unmistakable. Observers could point to important technological advances (such as the increasing use of electricity to drive spinning machines in the textile industry after 1905), to the high profits made by the 'staple' industries (see page 2), and to the growth of new industries like chemical engineering, cars, soap and confectionery. In particular, the economy seemed to boom between 1910 and 1913.

Contemporaries looked at Britain's economic performance in contrasting ways. This is not surprising: they were too close to events to achieve any real perspective, and so their opinions could only be impressionistic. Indeed it was impossible for them to judge the performance of the economy as a whole because reliable statistical evidence simply did not exist. National unemployment figures were not calculated, and nor was gross domestic product (GDP) – the sum value of all goods and services in the economy. Still less did they have authoritative evidence on Britain's past performance or on that of its foreign competitors.

b) The Period in Retrospect

Which group was correct, the optimists or the pessimists? This is a difficult question because historians too are bedevilled by the lack of accurate statistics. However, most historians judge that, because they are not mutually exclusive, both schools of thought were correct. There were positive and negative aspects to economic performance in these years.

By 1914 Britain still had a strong economy. It was easily the world's largest foreign investor, owning over 40 per cent of the world's foreign investment, a source of great wealth from dividends. Britain also owned most of the world's shipping and still produced a significant proportion of the world's manufactured goods – but it was a declining proportion, falling from around one-third of world output in 1900 to one-quarter in 1914. The economy was still growing, but the rate of growth was declining. Output was still rising after 1900 but not as quickly as previously. The American and German economies were growing much more quickly – probably twice as fast – between 1900 and 1913.

It is also true that there were technological advances in Britain, but perhaps even more significant was the degree to which such change did not occur. This was particularly the case in the 'staple' industries. Despite the fact that some machines were powered by electricity, on the whole the textile industry failed to modernise. The same was true of the coal industry, where production rose but productivity (output per worker) fell. Output from British pits had never been higher than in 1913, but never before had so many miners been employed. Whereas coal mining in America and Germany was undergoing mechanisation, in Britain coal was still being extracted by old-fashioned methods, largely by men wielding picks. In fact, output per miner in Britain fell by around 20 per cent between 1880 and 1914, as men had to work on progressively thinner coal seams. Around 1850 Britain had spearheaded technological development, but this was no longer the case. Instead Britain was lagging behind its main competitors in this important area.

In other ways too the British economy was no longer progressive. It was the Americans, not the British, who introduced 'conveyor-belt' techniques of mass production, as in Henry Ford's car factories after 1900. The Americans also introduced a 'high wage' economy: workers were paid enough to buy the goods they produced, thus ensuring a high demand that stimulated production. In Britain, in contrast, there was a 'low wage' economy, so that only rich and middle-class people could afford to buy other than very simple manufactured goods (and they relied so much on cheap domestic servants that their need for labour-saving goods was small). Thus the domestic market was very limited. Furthermore, it was the Americans and Germans who pioneered industry on a large scale, thus profiting from 'economies of scale' (the savings that can be made from bulk purchases and so on). In Britain factories were much smaller and so incurred relatively greater costs. Many industrialists in Britain were slow to adopt these new cost-cutting changes and also new and more efficient marketing techniques.

Some new industries were appearing in Britain before 1914, and this was a promising sign. Yet the staple industries were still dominant in the economy, and since their products were meeting increasing competition from abroad they could not maintain their share of world trade. Exports of electrical goods, vehicles and aircraft – typical 'new' products – accounted for only 2.2 per cent of British exports by value in 1913. In contrast, cotton, woollens, coal and iron and steel accounted for 51 per cent. In Germany and elsewhere governments provided subsidies to help new industries grow and flourish, but British governments did not. Because the industrial revolution had occurred 'from the bottom up' (as a result of the efforts of pioneering individuals rather than the actions of governments) people in Britain tended to place their trust in *laissez-faire*.

One positive aspect of the British economy was the financial expertise of the City of London. Its foreign investments and the financial services it offered to other nationals certainly produced high profits. Yet this should not disguise an important fact about the British economy in 1900–14. Britain was importing goods worth more than the goods it exported. The volume (and value) of British exports was growing, although more slowly than in earlier decades, but imports were growing even more rapidly. There was thus a deficit on the 'current account' – that is, the value of goods imported exceeded the value of goods exported. However, there was not an overall deficit, because on the 'capital account' so-called 'invisible exports' (profits from overseas investments and from financial transactions) more than compensated and so put the overall balance of payments in profit.

Overall, Britain was still an economically strong country in this period. It had in fact never been more prosperous. There was no decline in the sense of an absolute fall in production: indeed there was a very healthy absolute growth, averaging around two per cent a year. But the enormous lead over its rivals that once existed had been lost, and there had thus been a *relative* decline. Many historians see this as the most important theme of the period.

c) Britain's Relative Economic Decline

There has been an extensive debate among historians about the causes of Britain's relative decline. So far there has been little agreement. This is perhaps not surprising. After all, Britain's relative decline was not an 'event', which might have a fairly simply explanation. Rather, it was a long and complex process, affecting some sectors of the economy and parts of the country much more than others. Nevertheless, it is generally agreed that collectively the following factors form the basis for a credible explanation.

i) Britain's economic supremacy in the mid-nineteenth century did not stem from an abundance of raw materials or the size of its population. Nor, as many fondly imagined at the time, was it due to the natural superiority of British people. It was simply 'a happy accident' (see page 3). It was therefore very unlikely to last long. It was not difficult for rivals to copy the industrial processes first begun in Britain. Indeed other countries, by starting the industrial race after Britain, could invest in the most modern equipment, while many British factories had to make do with relatively old-fashioned industrial plant. This interpretation is sometimes called the 'early start' thesis.

ii) Countries with more natural advantages than Britain were very likely, sooner or later, to overtake British production totals. Both the USA and Germany had larger populations and more abundant raw materials. When Britain had been experiencing industrial boom, these rivals had been unable to complete effectively. The United States was embroiled in civil war between 1861 and 1865, while Germany did not even become a unified state until 1871; but from the 1880s onwards, they were both in a good position to forge ahead more rapidly than Britain.

iii) Britain was handicapped by the trading policies of its rivals. Its economy had grown strong during the era of free trade. With no restrictions on trade, Britain had been able to buy in the cheapest market and sell in the dearest. Other countries found it hard to develop their own industries when British goods were usually so much cheaper and more reliable that they sold better than locally produced ones. But from the 1880s most trading nations imposed protective tariffs on incoming foreign goods, making them more expensive, and so gave a fillip to local industries. Britain was alone amongst the leading trading nations in sticking to free trade.

iv) Perhaps too much capital went abroad. On average, between 1870 and 1914, 5.2 per cent of Britain's gross domestic product was invested abroad, and by 1914 £4,000 million was invested overseas. In some years more was invested abroad than at home, and indeed in 1911–13 twice as much went overseas. Perhaps this export of capital hindered domestic growth by starving British industry of finance; certainly it hastened the industrialisation of rivals.

v) Some historians have argued that a root cause of Britain's failure to maintain its industrial lead was the development of an 'anti-enterprise culture'. There is no doubt that the education system was very poorly geared to the needs of industry. It gave prominence to the classics (Latin and Greek) and competitive sport, and there was not sufficient scientific research or technical education. By 1913 Germany produced six times as many science graduates as Britain. Perhaps the 'industrial spirit' never fully gripped the British people, trade and industry often being considered vulgar and socially demeaning.

Historians have often divided these causes of Britain's relative decline into the 'economic' and the 'social and psychological'. Another useful division is the 'avoidable' and the 'unavoidable'. Certainly some economic decline was inevitable. There was no chance that Britain could hold on indefinitely to the enormous lead which it had established in the middle of the nineteenth century due to special and short-lived circumstances. A measure of economic decline, in comparison with rivals such as the USA and Germany, was therefore certain. The key question was not whether Britain would decline, relative to its rivals, but how long and how steep this decline would be. Would British industry be technologically modernised? Would the old staple industries continue to dominate the British economy, or could other sectors produce new growth and productivity? Would 'invisible exports' continue to compensate for the imbalance between exports and imports?

A trend towards relative decline had been established by 1914, but the significance of that trend – how it would affect the future and form part of a larger pattern – was far from certain.

4 Trade Unions and the Law, 1900–14

> **KEY ISSUE** Why had the attack on trade union powers been defeated by 1914?

Clearly the industrialisation of Britain in the nineteenth century had produced not only great wealth but also exploitation and gross disparities of income. Trade unions had grown up to combat this inequality and to secure a better deal – higher wages and improved conditions of work – for their members. By the end of the nineteenth century the unions had achieved recognition from the state (see page 5), but their exact position in law was still a matter for controversy.

In 1900 the unions, together with a number of small socialist societies, founded the Labour Representation Committee, which became known as the Labour Party from 1906. Many of the most radical union leaders wanted not merely to secure piecemeal improvements in particular industries but, in the words of one of them, 'to stamp out poverty from the land'. They realised that this necessitated political as well as economic action. Some other union leaders, wishing to stay out of politics, disapproved of this move: they were suspicious of ideas like 'socialism' and 'equality' and instead wished to maintain wage differentials between separate groups of workers. Yet, on the whole, the founding of the Labour Party seemed a sign that the trade unions were to become more influential than ever before. But first there were challenges and setbacks.

a) The Taff Vale Case, 1900–2

Trade union success at the end of the nineteenth century, together with the growing confrontational atmosphere between employers and unions in the 1890s, provoked a backlash from those who felt that unions were becoming too powerful. In 1901 *The Times* argued that trade unions, by their restrictive practices, were responsible for Britain's weakening industrial position against foreign competition. A *Daily Mail* headline put it even more bluntly: 'American Furniture in England: A further indictment of the trade unions'.

Some working men also disapproved of the new militant stand the unions were taking and formed the National Free Labour Association. This was essentially a team of men prepared to act as strike-breakers by taking over the work of men on strike. In 1900 members of the association were taken on by the Taff Vale railway company of South Wales, whose own employees were on strike. The local union fought back. Some strikers greased the railway track on inclines so that trains carrying 'blacklegs' could not reach their destination. Others organised picketing and tried to persuade the Association members not to work. The company manager then took the issue to the courts, claiming damages from the union for inducement to breach of contract. The strike itself was soon over, but the legal case dragged on until 1902 when the House of Lords (the highest court in the land) ruled that the union would have to pay damages of £23,000 to the company, plus legal costs of £19,000.

This judgement was a severe blow. It has been called a 'judicial *coup d'état*' which made strikes 'for all practical purposes absolutely illegal'. It followed a legal ruling that seemed to forbid peaceful picketing and preceded by only a fortnight another which again awarded damages against a union involved in a strike. Unions were far more reluctant to call strikes, now that their funds might be confiscated in damages. Another result was that more trade unionists than before saw the need for a change in the law and therefore pinned their hopes on the Labour Party. However, the next setback seemed to cast doubts upon whether unions would even be allowed to support Labour.

b) The Osborne Judgement, 1909

A railway employee, Walter Osborne, a Liberal supporter, disliked the fact that a portion of his union fees went to help finance the Labour Party. Finding wealthy Liberal and Conservative backers, he took his case to the courts, and eventually the House of Lords ruled in his favour, deciding that trade unions could no longer spend money for political purposes. The unions were now unable to support the Labour Party with donations from union fees. Nor could they pay the political expenses of Labour or trade union candidates in elections.

The Taff Vale ruling meant that the unions could not involve themselves in effective industrial action; the Osborne Judgement ruled out effective political action. Some feared – and other hoped – that British trade unions would decline in importance.

Yet by 1914 the unions were more powerful than ever. Their success was due in part to the general elections of 1906 and 1910. In 1906 the Liberals achieved a great victory and, encouraged by Labour MPs, passed the 1906 Trade Disputes Act, which has been called 'the essential charter of trade unionism'. It legalised peaceful picketing and reversed the Taff Vale judgement, so that unions could no longer be sued for damages caused by strikes. The two elections of 1910 were much closer-run affairs. The Liberals were only kept in office by their allies, including Labour, and as a result Labour MPs were in a position to insist on further reforms. In 1911 payment for MPs was agreed, each member of the House of Commons receiving an annual salary of £400. It was henceforth much easier for trade unionists and working men generally to become MPs. Then, in 1913, the Trade Union Act reversed the Osborne Judgement. Trade unions could now impose a 'political levy' on their members, providing that, in a ballot, over half the members of a union accepted the proposal and providing also that those who did not wish to pay the levy were given the opportunity to 'contract out' of doing so.

5 Waves of Industrial Unrest, 1908–14

> **KEY ISSUES** Why did so many strikes occur from 1908 onwards. What was the significance of this industrial militancy?

a) What Happened

The years before the First World War saw not only an important strengthening of the unions' legal position but also a number of prolonged and bitter strikes. It was a period of unprecedented 'labour unrest'. Lenin, the Russian revolutionary, judged that British workers had embarked on 'the great heroic struggle for a new system of society'.

Between 1900 and 1907 there had been few major strikes in Britain. The average number of days lost in this period had been about 2.75 million per year. But in 1908 that figure jumped to almost 11 million, and in 1912 it reached a massive 41 million. In 1911 there were prolonged strikes by the dockers and seamen in support of a claim for higher wages. In Liverpool, where food supplies could pass through pickets only with a military escort, violence broke out. One policeman was killed and two men were shot by soldiers. The Lord Mayor of Liverpool feared that there would be a revolution, and warships were moored in the Mersey with their guns trained on the city. In the same year there was the first national strike on the railways in Britain's history. But perhaps the greatest trouble occurred in the mines.

A three-month strike took place in the Northumberland and Durham coalfields in 1910, to be followed shortly afterwards by a ten-month strike in South Wales, when the owners refused to give miners extra pay for working difficult seams. 'Blackleg' labour was used, and soon miners were fighting with police. Eventually cavalry was sent to Tonypandy, where one miner was killed. In Llanelli two more were killed (one of whom was simply watching from his back garden as rioters threw stones at a train). Both these miners' strikes failed, but in March 1912 the Miners' Federation of Great Britain called a national strike to secure a minimum wage for all miners. One historian has called this strike 'the biggest stoppage the world had yet seen'. This time victory was achieved. Already the Liberal government had, in 1908, legislated to give the miners an eight-hour day; now it passed the Coal Mines Act of 1912. This established a system for setting minimum wages in the various coal mining districts. There was no single national minimum wage, but miners' leaders had achieved most of what they wanted and so recommended a return to work.

Yet this was not an end to strikes or industrial violence. In the Dublin transport strike of 1913, clashes between police and strikers developed into riots in which hundreds were injured and two men died of fractured skulls. It has been said that 'frightened police going berserk in baton charges were almost a commonplace' in the five years before the war.

b) Explanations

There are two main ways of explaining this wave of strikes. The first sees industrial activity as stemming from a new mood of political militancy among British workers and judges that, but for the outbreak of the First World War in 1914, workers might well have organised a general strike – and perhaps a revolution. The second considers the industrial disputes to be less significant in that they had basically economic origins and motivations that had largely run their course before the war began.

i) The Influence of Syndicalism

Many journalists were convinced that the wave of strikes was a portent of revolution. In 1911 Winston Churchill, the Home Secretary, said that Britain was about to be 'hurled into an abyss of horror', and the following year *The Times* judged the coal strike to be 'the greatest catastrophe that has threatened the country since the Spanish Armada'. Was this an over-reaction, or were the strikes indeed a sign of something more than economic discontent?

It has often been said that behind the workers' militancy lay the doctrine of syndicalism. This was a theory advocated by the French writer Georges Sorel. Like most socialists, Sorel believed that the interests of the owners of industry and of the workers were diametrically opposed. What distinguished his thinking was a new stress on the use of 'direct action' by workers to overthrow capitalism. He believed that workers in the same industry should be encouraged to join a single large union, so that strikes would be all the more complete and effective. In the end, such unions would cover every sector of industry. Strikes were to be used as a political weapon against the capitalists and, eventually, a general strike would take place which would overthrow capitalism altogether and lead to workers' control of industry.

The most important British convert to syndicalism was Tom Mann, one of the key figures in the history of British trade unionism. Already, in 1889, he had taken a leading role in the successful London dock strike (see page 5), when he had insisted that the true union policy should be one of aggression against the capitalists. Now, in 1910, he began to publish a radical monthly journal, the *Industrial Syndicalist*, and formed the National Transport Workers' Federation, very much the sort of large-scale union advocated by syndicalism. He also helped organise the dock strikes of the following year, urging strikers not to be 'too mealy-mouthed over law and order'. There were others too who were influenced by syndicalism. In South Wales during the disputes of 1912 a group of miners produced *The Miners' Next Step*, which clearly bore a syndicalist imprint:

1 Alliances [are] to be formed, and trade organisations fostered, with a view to steps being taken, to amalgamate all workers into one National and International union, to work for the taking over of all industries, by the workers themselves ...

5 The Irritation strike depends for its successful adoption, on the men holding clearly the point of view, that their interests and the employers [*sic*] are necessarily hostile. Further, that the employer is vulnerable only in one place, his profits! Therefore if the men wish to bring effective pressure to bear, they must use methods which tend to reduce

10 profits. One way of doing this is to decrease production, while continuing to work ...

Our objective begins to take shape before your eyes. Every industry thoroughly organised, in the first place, to gain control of, and then administer, that industry. The co-ordination of all industries on a

15 Central Production Board ... who will issue its demands on the different departments of industry, leaving the men themselves to determine under what conditions and how, the work shall be done. This would mean real democracy in real life, making for real manhood and womanhood. Any other form of democracy is a delusion and a snare.

This document has been called 'the classic statement of British syndicalism'.

A further sign of syndicalist influence may have appeared in 1914. Already several groups of unions had amalgamated, and now the 'triple alliance' was formed out of three of the largest federations of workers – the miners, the railwaymen and the transport workers. The power of these workers seemed such that they might use their combined industrial muscle to extract any concessions from their employers. Some have argued that the alliance's intention to launch a general strike on Britain was only averted by the outbreak of the First World War.

ii) Economic Causes of Unrest

Debate among the experts is continuing, but probably most historians now think that the influence of syndicalism on British industrial unrest was exaggerated by the press. It has been pointed out that, although some individuals like Tom Mann and the South Wales miners were clearly influenced by syndicalism, many more were not. According to this interpretation, the wave of strikes after 1908 can be satisfactorily explained partly by political circumstances, but primarily by economic factors.

In the few years before 1906 there were relatively few strikes in

Britain. This was mainly due to the Taff Vale ruling, which made union leaders cautious about taking industrial action. After 1906 and the Trade Disputes Act there were likely to be more strikes – especially since economic grievances were beginning to multiply. In the final decades of the previous century prices had been falling, and therefore as long as union leaders could maintain wages at their existing levels their members had been better off. But now prices began to rise. This inflation put a great strain on industrial relations. Union leaders would have to secure pay rises simply in order for the standard of living of their men to remain stationary. Rising prices are seen by several historians as the key to the wave of strikes; and it follows from this that trade unionists, far from wanting to overthrow capitalism, merely wished to prevent a deterioration in the living standards of their members. Their actions, which some have called 'the great offensive', were primarily defensive. Although experts dispute the precise rate of inflation, it seems likely that it was only in 1914, after prolonged strikes, that real wages returned to their 1909 level.

The economy is also said to explain another factor that helped produce strikes. Trade began to improve and the economy to expand after 1908. In particular the years 1911–13 have been called the 'great boom'. More people were employed, and in this situation not only did greater numbers join trade unions – so that total union membership grew from 2.4 million in 1910 to 4.1 million in 1913 – but there were fewer unemployed people to act as strike-breakers. Unions are always at an advantage when the 'trade cycle' (see pages 57–8) is improving. Profits are then higher, and employers can generally afford to pay their workers better wages.

Furthermore there were special circumstances that explain particular disputes. In the coal industry, for instance, owners were reluctant to give higher wages because of the extra costs produced by government legislation, which insisted on new safety regulations and on a maximum working day of eight hours. On the railways, where costs were rising, the government had pegged freight rates by an Act of Parliament. The result was that higher costs could not be reflected in higher prices, and so the firms reacted by introducing larger engines and rolling stock. As a result, many men found themselves shovelling twice as much coal for no increase in wages – a sure recipe for industrial friction.

6 Conclusion: a Gathering Storm?

> **KEY ISSUE** How close to revolution was Britain before 1914?

a) The 'Golden Age'

Clearly the idea of a 'golden age' is a subjective one. No doubt there were many among the rich upper classes who gloried in their affluence and freedom. Many members of the middle classes also had greater prosperity than ever before. A larger number were to look back nostalgically on the 1900–14 era: after the horrors of war it seemed a sort of Eden from which the British had been rudely expelled. Yet the idea that, for British society as a whole, the Edwardian period had been some sort of idyll cannot be accepted. There was stark poverty, and a substantial proportion of the population – even while working excessively long hours – did not earn enough to live healthily. Many Edwardians were unhappy about the state of their society, and this was a period of acute social friction.

On the other hand, we should not exaggerate the miseries of Edwardian society or underestimate the degree to which progress had been made. Appalling though the conditions Rowntree described in York in 1901 undoubtedly were, they pale in comparison with earlier surveys, such as that published by Engels on Manchester in 1845. There were also some improvements, prompted partly by government legislation. Class conflict undoubtedly existed, but there was class collaboration as well. Pro-monarchical and pro-imperial sentiment transcended, and bound together, the classes. At Robert Roberts's school in Salford, teachers 'spelled out patriotism among us with a fervour that with some verged on the religious ... We drew union jacks, hung classrooms with flags of the Dominions and gazed with pride as they pointed out those massed areas of red on the world map.' To the downtrodden in Britain was preached the comforting doctrine that a Briton was worth a dozen foreigners; and Britons of all classes answered the call to fight 'for king and country' in 1914. Even the suffragettes rallied to the cause (see pages 45–9 for the history of the women's movement).

b) Strikes

The years before the First World War certainly constituted a menacing period industrially. There was a definite militancy among many British workers, for whom trade union leaders were often too moderate. Indeed it was said by the government's industrial relations expert, Sir George Askwith, that 'often there was more difference between the men and their leaders than between the latter and the employers'. It was thus, to some extent, a three-cornered contest: men versus unions versus employers. Owing partly to the growing size of many unions, a gulf began to open up between ordinary workers and their national leaders, several of whom had also become Members of Parliament. The result was that shop-floor grievances led to 'unofficial' strikes (that is, those not supported and organised by the unions). Small wonder that even Conservative politicians wished to see a stronger trade union movement: it was thought that unions, if well organised and disciplined, would lessen the influence of the militants and so reduce the number of strikes.

Militancy undoubtedly existed, but it did not necessarily constitute a real challenge to the government of the day. There is still room for doubt about the causes of the strikes of the period, especially since so little is known of many of them, but on balance it seems that a stronger case can be made out for the wave of strikes having primarily economic rather than political or syndicalist origins. Admittedly there was an unusual amount of violence in the strikes of 1910–12, but this may well have been due to government tactics. On several occasions the Home Secretary waived the normal rules and sent troops to disputes when the local authorities had not requested assistance. We should also bear in mind that some strikes were due to the intransigence of employers – many of whom wished to crush the unions – and to the lack of any widely accepted procedures for settling disputes.

The government's expert on industrial relations, Sir George Askwith, judged in a speech in 1913 that the rash of strikes had a number of causes:

1 There is a spirit abroad of unrest, of movement, a spirit and a desire of improvement, of alteration. We are in, perhaps, as quick an age of transition as there has been for many generations past. The causes of this are manifold. I am only going to indicate a few. One is that the school-
5 master has been abroad in the land, and that, as education improves, the more a man wishes to get to a better and higher position ... Again, every man, whatever the actual cost of his livelihood may be, if he has arrived at a particular standard of life, not only desires to improve it, but also would struggle hard before he would give it up. When you
10 come to certain standards of wages and livelihood, and find that particular things that you particularly use rise greatly in price, it affects the amenities of life and the margin of life to such an extent that there is disenchantment and a desire to keep to the standard which may have been achieved. Then there is the spirit of movement throughout the
15 world. We quicken day by day means of transport ...

In addition to that you have in this country for some years past what I may call political equality. One man's vote is as good as another ... If a man has got educated up to the view of considering himself politically equal to another man, he is far more anxious to achieve a greater
20 amount of economic equality; a desire to reach that economic equality must necessarily exist in his mind ... That, shortly, sums up some of the reasons why there is unrest, unrest that nobody can be surprised at, and which is bound to continue. Are men to remain in a backwater and do nothing ...?

What of the general strike that some insist would have occurred in 1914? It seems to have been only a bare possibility. First, rather than strikes approaching a climax in the summer of 1914, there was a calming of the situation in 1913 and the first six months of 1914. Almost 41 million working days were lost in 1912, but in 1913 the total fell to just under ten million, with virtually the same figure for 1914. Significantly, *The Miners' Next Step* was issued when militancy had already reached its height. It did not inspire further industrial action. In fact, as the syndicalist influence became more pronounced in South Wales, union membership there fell off, against the national trend.

Secondly, the 'triple alliance' was formed in the spring of 1914 not to spearhead a general strike but to avoid the need for strikes. The terms of the alliance did not allow its leaders simply to call a strike: instead union members had to be consulted, and in some cases balloted – a lengthy and complicated procedure. The president of the Railwaymen's union judged that the alliance 'is neither revolutionary nor Syndicalist. It is a force which is not intended to be used indiscriminately or frivolously'. One expert has commented that 'The attraction of the alliance … lay in the promise of bloodless battles'. In short, the leaders of the alliance probably hoped to achieve their objectives by bluff alone. Union leaders were prepared to use syndicalist slogans ('direct action', 'the general strike', 'workers' control of industry'), but syndicalism was not a dominant strand in union thinking.

Several writers, and especially George Dangerfield, have painted a picture of a nation ripe for revolution in 1914, one cataclysm only averted by an alternative cataclysm, the First World War. They have argued that not only industrial relations but the troubles in Ireland and the activities of the suffragettes pointed to violent revolution. 'Liberal England' was dying: instead of solving problems by discussion and reason, people were taking direct action. But the main problem with this view is that no one has managed to show convincingly that connections existed between these three separate, and in many ways dissimilar, problems. Of course it is impossible to prove that a civil war or revolution might not have occurred but for the start of the war. But the onus must surely be on those who seek to show that revolution was brewing to demonstrate their case convincingly. So far they have not done so.

Was there a 'gathering storm' in industrial relations from 1908 to 1914? There were industrial problems in plenty, and the strikes in 1910–12 must be considered industrial storms of the first magnitude. But those who employ this phrase about 1908–14 are implying that the squalls before 1914 were merely a prelude to a much larger storm, that the storm clouds were gathering for an almighty downpour. Yet it seems that the worst was over by 1914. Certainly the press thought so, and the government needed to intervene less in industrial disputes after 1912. The clouds had not been dispelled, but the forecast was for showers or drizzle rather than storms.

b) The Economy

If industrial relations were not predestined to produce catastrophe by 1914, what of the economy as a whole? Was Britain heading downhill at breakneck speed? Were the clouds gathering for an economic storm? Economic commentators at the time were sharply divided on this issue. While articles in *The Times* spoke of a 'crisis of industry' and pessimists predicted calamity, others looked forward to steady progress and increasing prosperity. Historians have tended to mirror this dichotomy of views.

Some writers have stressed the negative features of these years, and in particular the fact that Britain was declining relative to its major competitors. There were certainly problems for the British economy. Almost everywhere, including in its own domestic market, British goods faced intense competition, and often foreign markets were defended by protective tariffs. New manufactured goods were being produced, but their value was small in comparison with the economy as a whole, and Britain's exports relied overmuch on staple industries which were not being modernised and whose products were able to command only a diminishing share of world trade. Indeed, perhaps the most worrying of all Britain's failures was its inability to remain at the forefront of technological innovation. Britain had developed every major new technique in steel manufacture in the nineteenth century, and yet failed to apply most of them to its own steel industry. (For instance, the techniques pioneered by Sidney Gilchrist-Thomas in 1877–8 helped the French and Germans far more than his countrymen.) Britain's steel and railway industries in the 1900s have been called outdated 'industrial dinosaurs'. One historian has judged that, because of its failure to modernise, the world's 'leading and most dynamic economy' was quickly being transformed into 'the most sluggish and conservative'. The implication of this view is that decline was so steep that it could not be halted.

Yet more optimistic historians counter that it was only to be expected that Britain would be overtaken by two larger and naturally richer states, the USA and Germany. The far more significant issue was whether Britain would be overtaken by countries with similar resources and population size, such as France, and by 1914 there were few signs that this was likely to happen. The French achieved only a marginally higher rate of manufacturing growth than Britain between 1900 and 1913. If such a rate continued in the future, Britain would still be economically the much stronger for generations. Admittedly there were problems for the economy, but these did not seem insuperable. Of Britain's exports, 35 per cent went to Europe, despite tariffs. Although Britain's share of world trade was diminishing, world trade was expanding rapidly, and so in absolute terms British goods were selling in greater quantities that ever before. The staple industries were still making very healthy profits. 'New industries' may have accounted for only a relatively small share of the total economy, but there was no reason to suppose that they would not grow in the future. And, despite balance of trade problems, 'invisible exports' were remarkably lucrative. It has been argued that there were good reasons to believe that Britain was adjusting successfully to new international market forces.

Clearly the economic record before the war was mixed. Therefore it would be unwise to take an extreme 'optimistic' or 'pessimistic' viewpoint about Britain's future economic prospects. Britain was facing severe economic problems, but the country was still prosperous and there were numerous signs of material improvement for the British people. Would the new climate of international economic competition have an ultimately bracing or depressing effect on Britain? This was the key question, and it was one that could only be decided by future developments. A trend towards relative decline had certainly been established in 1914, but the significance of this trend would depend on Britain's economic performance over a much longer period. The longer-term future had not been predetermined by these years. There were economic problems ahead, but there was surely no 'gathering storm' in the sense that an inevitable economic catastrophe was brewing. Only the future could decide whether or when Britain's relative decline would end.

Perhaps the most important clouds on the horizon in 1908-14 stemmed from the menacing international situation. For years crises between the Great Powers in Europe had been threatening to unleash war. Britain's economy was, more than any other country's, integrated with that of the world. Britain traded more – and earned more from world commerce, both 'visible' and 'invisible' – than any other country. It also relied on an exceptionally high level of imports: over 50 per cent of food consumed in Britain was imported, as well as over 50 per cent of the raw materials used by industry. In a sense therefore, Britain, the world's largest creditor nation (lending more money than any other country), was also a dependent nation. It had far more to lose from war, and especially such a war as the Great War turned out to be.

Summary Diagrams
1900–14: The Gathering Storm?

1900   **Trade unionism**   **1914**

Trade unions: Two million members

Taff Vale 1902

Trade Disputes Act 1906

Trade unions: Four million members

Anti-trade union

Pro-trade union

Osborne Judgement 1909

Trade Union Act 1913

Waves of Labour unrest, 1908–14: syndicalist offensive or defensive reaction to price rises?

Britain's economy

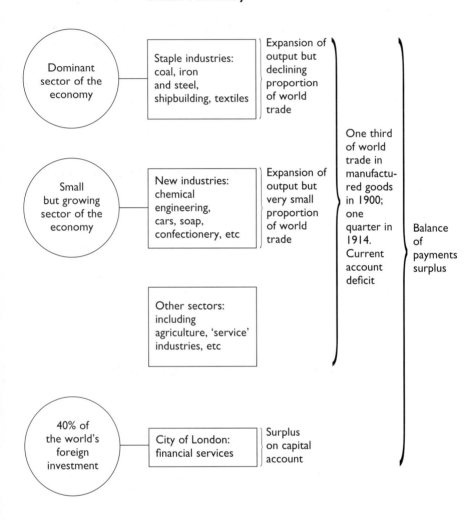

Working on Chapter 2

You need to make fairly full notes on this chapter, especially since the trends of the period 1900–14 were important for the issues covered later in this book. The headings and sub-headings in the text should help you to organise the material. (For a discussion of women's roles in British society before 1914, see pages 45–8 of the next chapter.)

Make a conscious effort to distinguish between 'facts' and 'interpretations' in your notes.

With factual material, especially statistics, remember that you do not need to copy down information in its entirety: instead you should express evidence in a form which you will be able to remember. At its most basic, this can mean that you note down mere trends, e.g. whether production was increasing or decreasing. Or you can express a percentage in approximate terms: 2.2 per cent can be rendered as 'just over two per cent', 23 per cent can be termed 'almost a quarter', and so on. There is no golden rule, except perhaps that you should tailor your notes to suit yourself.

As for interpretation, the most important thing initially is to grasp the essential ideas rather than the details. The first thing to do is to write down a very brief summary (normally no more than one sentence) of the interpretation in your own words. Then you may add extra details and illustrations if you wish to. In the final section of your notes (the conclusion), you should try to formulate your own verdicts.

One final suggestion: you may already have found yourself picking out certain 'technical' terms and making a note of what they mean. If you have not, it might be a good idea to do so. Keep this personal glossary (a collection of definitions) separate from your other notes. Such terms as 'relative decline', 'real wages', 'productivity' and others might be included at this stage. Add to your list as you read succeeding chapters.

Answering structured and essay questions on Chapter 2

A typical structured question on this period is as follows:

a) What were the sources of Britain's economic prosperity around 1910?
b) Why were some Britons anxious about Britain's economic future at that time?

A structured question is not an essay; and hence there is no need to observe all the conventions of a good essay. Instead, while avoiding writing notes, you should answer each part of the questions directly and concisely. Use any mark-scheme as a guide as to how much time to devote to each part. Do read the whole question before attempting to answer each part. For instance, for a) above you might be tempted to qualify the sources of prosperity by introducing some of the weaknesses of the economy – but clearly this information will only score points if included in b).

Many essay questions cover a wider period than 1900–14, but it is worth considering two on these years alone:

1. Why was there so much industrial unrest in the period 1900–14?
2. To what extent was the period between 1900 and 1914 one of steep economic decline for Great Britain?

The golden rule for writing history essays is simple – it is to 'answer the question, the whole question and nothing but the question'. No marks can be awarded for irrelevant material. The key to a good essay is often the first paragraph: in this you should establish the precise meaning of the question (including its component terms) as well as breaking it down into smaller, more manageable issues, each of which you will later develop into a whole paragraph. You can also outline your basic argument. Detailed advice on planning opening paragraphs is given in a companion volume to this one, *Britain: Domestic Policies, 1918–39*. See especially pages 39–40 of the second edition.

Attempt a first paragraph for each of the two questions above. Why do you think the wording of the second question stresses decline 'for' – rather than 'in' Britain? How will you define 'steep' in this question?

Another vital part of the essay – indeed its culmination – is the final paragraph. In this you should be attempting to do several things:

i) Having dealt with discrete aspects of the question in the middle paragraphs, you should now be recapping, drawing together the threads of your argument, and so returning to the whole question.

ii) You should be commenting on the various interpretations or 'schools of thought' relevant to the issue in the title and you should be giving your opinion on the central issue in the question set. Do not be afraid of giving *your* view: after all, this is what the question asks for. On the other hand, there is no need to use the words 'in my opinion' since your view should stem from the evidence you have brought forward. A merely personal view will not sound authoritative.

iii) Above all, you must hammer home your conclusion. So refer back to the original question and answer it as succinctly and clearly as you can. That does not mean that you have to be one-sided or audacious and shocking: you can be as judicious and cautious as you like. But whatever view you put forward, it must be clearly and forcefully expressed. Faint heart never won fair mark! In a conclusion, you must be conclusive.

Another way of considering this key area is to be aware of what you should not do. Do not load the paragraph down with factual information. Instead, you should be drawing logical conclusions from the facts brought forward in earlier paragraphs. Do not merely repeat what you have said already in the essay. And do not spring some new and unexpected idea that you have just thought of on the reader: more often than not, this will contradict views expressed earlier in the essay. The conclusion should stem logically from the rest of the essay. Nor should you 'look forward' and introduce another topic. For instance, you should not, having looked at 1900–14, then go on to write a brief introduction to 1914–18. Such irrelevancy – while common enough amongst examinees – actually loses marks rather than scores them.

You might practise writing brief conclusions, say six to eight lines, for both of the above essay titles. Take your time over this and do not be satisfied until you are sure your mini-conclusion cannot be improved upon. (It may seem paradoxical or even perverse to start at the end, but this is not a bad way of beginning preparations for writing an essay. It will prevent inconsistency, and in addition it should ensure that the essay is leading somewhere.)

Source-based questions on Chapter 2

1. Causes of Conflict
Read the extracts from *The Miners' Next Step* on page 24 and from the speech by Sir George Askwith on page 27 and answer the following questions:

a) What aspects of *The Miners' Next Step* could be called 'syndicalist'? Explain your answer. (*5 marks*)

b) What is missing from the full syndicalist programme? (*3 marks*)

c) Explain how, in the authors' opinion, the 'irritation strike' would further the cause of the workers. (*2 marks*)

d) What do you think Askwith meant by an 'age of transition' (lines 2–3)? (*2 marks*)

e) Explain his references to the influence of i) 'the schoolmaster' (lines 4–5), and ii) 'means of transport' (line 15). (*4 marks*)

f) Is he saying, on balance, that strikers wanted to improve or merely to protect their standard of living? Explain your answer. (*4 marks*)

g) Using these two documents and your own knowledge, judge how far these two sources explain the causes of the wave of strikes. (*12 marks*)

3 The First World War

POINTS TO CONSIDER

It is often said that war is the 'locomotive of history' – that it is what drives it along. Certainly the First World War helped to produce major changes in British government, society, the economy and industrial relations. You have to be aware of these changes and also to try to measure their importance, while resisting the temptation to exaggerate their significance. Did they speed up changes that were already under way, or did they produce an entirely new situation? Were their effects important only for the 1914–18 period or were they more long-lasting?

KEY DATES

1897	National Union of Women's Suffrage Societies founded by Millicent Fawcett.
1903	The Women's Social and Political Union founded by Emmeline Pankhurst.
1914 August	Outbreak of war.
1915	Strikes on the Clyde.
March	'Treasury Agreement'.
May	Lloyd George became Minister of Munitions.
July	Munitions of War Act, banning strikes and making dilution compulsory.
1916 Dec	Lloyd George became Prime Minister.
1917	Engineering strikes in Coventry, Manchester and Sheffield.
1918	6 million trade union members.
11 Nov	End of the war.

The outbreak of war in August 1914 produced immediate changes. Almost overnight, British society became more united in the face of a common enemy. Industrial relations certainly improved. Some socialists, hoping that the British would refuse to fight against their fellow workers from Germany, called for a general strike. A left-wing paper insisted that only the class war was worth waging and that the workers had no country. Were not all workers, of whatever nationality, members of the same exploited class? Were they not, in fact, all brothers? The answer forthcoming was in the negative, as men flocked to enlist. If civil war was a possibility in July 1914, revolution was quickly forgotten in August.

The government assumed that the war would be won by Christmas. This was a great error, for the destructive power of modern weaponry ruled out an early victory for either side. Technological advance in the nineteenth century had produced weapons of tremendous destructive power – not only reliable and accurate long-range rifles but also machine guns, able to fire 50 bullets a second. These new weapons, while too bulky to be easily carried, were especially powerful in defence, and the First World War therefore turned out to be a conflict marked by huge casualties in which defensive forces played a central role. The bulk of the fighting took place in France, on the western front: troops dug themselves in, and though both sides made periodic attacks and suffered spectacular losses, very little territory could be taken. After November 1914 the 'front line' was not to move by ten miles in any direction for the next three years. It was a long and destructive war of attrition.

The armies of Europe had an insatiable demand for munitions. As a result, this was a war not just between armies but between economies: it was a producers' war and an engineers' war, as well as a soldiers'. Britain's economy had to be put on a war footing and production maximised. The war tested all aspects of the British economy to the full – not only its industrial production but also its agriculture, its trade and its finance. Never before had Britain's economic performance been of such momentous significance.

The 'front line' depended on the 'home front'. It was therefore a 'total war'. All were involved, civilians as well as soldiers, women as well as men. Good industrial relations also mattered more than ever before. Strikes in British industry could literally be a matter of life and death for those fighting in France. There had to be substantial class collaboration, and also collaboration between the sexes. But if all were involved, not all were involved to quite the same degree, and some historians – basing their views on a 'Military Participation Ratio' – believe that the amount of change experienced by each particular group reflected its involvement in the war. Theories like these must be tested by a study of what happened.

1 The Wartime Economy

> **KEY ISSUES** What economic changes were brought about by the war? How effectively did the economy perform? How was the war paid for?

a) State Control

At first it was assumed that private enterprise would supply the materials needed for the successful prosecution of the war; but, as hopes of an early victory declined, the effects of war not only disrupted normal party politics but necessitated government intervention to maximise production.

The war produced political turmoil. In 1915 Prime Minister

Asquith formed a coalition government, and the following year he was replaced as premier by Lloyd George, who gave new impetus to the direction of the war. Lloyd George's methods were not orthodox, but he did manage to get things done. A contemporary summed him up: the new Prime Minister 'cares nothing for precedents and knows no principles, but he has fire in his belly, and that is what we want'. Before the war he had been the Liberal least committed to *laissez-faire*, and now he ended it completely. He believed that war was too serious a business to be left to free market forces.

At the start of the war the government, realising the vital importance of transport in modern warfare, took control of Britain's railway system. The following year a Ministry of Munitions was created: for the first time the State manufactured arms and ammunition. Although this ministry may not have been run with quite the efficiency and precision that Lloyd George, its first minister, later implied in his memoirs, it did open 60 new armaments factories by the end of 1915, and by the end of the war it had over three million workers under its direction. One control seemed to lead to another, as the government sought to increase Britain's economic efficiency in this increasingly desperate and destructive war. Control of shipping and the mines was added to the railways, and soon the government had banned strikes, introduced conscription to the army and rationed food. By the summer of 1918 the government virtually controlled the whole of British industry, as well as importing 90 per cent of goods that entered the country and marketing 80 per cent of the food consumed at home. Mistakes were undoubtedly made, but on the whole British resources were effectively mobilised to aid the war effort. Just over 60 per cent of the entire work force became directly engaged in war work.

The government had the difficult task of providing troops for the army while at the same time maintaining a large enough workforce to produce the war material that was required. The army expanded rapidly. By the end of 1914 over one million men had volunteered, far more than had been expected. As a result, many had no weapons and drilled with wooden rifles. By the end of 1915 there were 2.5 million in the armed forces, including many skilled craftsmen who could not really be spared from industry. In 1916 therefore a form of military conscription was introduced which enabled the army to expand while retaining key workers for the home front. This system was intensified the following year, and in the spring of 1918 conscription was extended to include men up to the age of 50. In the final year of war, despite heavy casualties, there were about 4 million men in the armed forces. A massive 46 per cent of all workers were then in the army.

We have to ask, in the light of this enormous military expansion, how Britain's industry was manned. (Perhaps we should say 'personned', since more women worked in industry than ever before during the war, see page 48.) The British economy provided jobs for an extra two and a half million people during the war. Most of these were women, entering paid employment for the first time. The remainder were men who put off retirement or who had previously been unemployed, or children under 14 who took on full-time jobs. The result was a gratifying one for the government: the size of the domestic workforce declined by only about one million, despite massive recruitment to the army. A reasonable balance had been struck between the needs of the army and the requirements of industry.

Statistics illustrate the gigantic war effort of the British. 187 million shells were manufactured and sent to France; and whereas in 1914 274 machine guns were made, in 1918 total output was over 120,000. In addition, clothing and footwear for the troops were produced on a vast scale. For example, 45 million pairs of boots and 33 million jackets were sent to the front.

b) Paying for the War

In addition, the government had other and scarcely less important concerns. How was the vast wartime effort to be paid for? Money as well as manpower was vital. The cost of the war in monetary terms was enormous. In 1913 the government had spent just under £200 million, slightly less than it raised in taxation. The budget was therefore balanced. But now the government had to spend more than ever before. By 1917 £7 million was being expended on the war every day. (In a single day in September 1918, the British fired 943,000 shells costing a massive £3.8 million!) In total in 1918 the government spent over £2,500 million while raising less than £900 million in taxation, thus creating a massive budget deficit.

During the war the British people were taxed much more highly than ever before. Indirect taxes (taxes on the purchase of goods) could not be raised by large amounts, since this would only cause inflation and fuel wage claims. But direct taxation was another matter, and the standard rate of tax was increased from about 6 to 25 per cent, while over 6 million more people became eligible to pay it. Yet despite this, taxes paid for only about 30 per cent of the cost of the war (a relatively high proportion in international terms: the Germans raised only half this percentage from taxation). The rest of the money was raised by selling overseas assets (estimates of the proportion sold vary from 10 to 25 per cent of overseas investments), by the sale of government bonds to the public, and by borrowing from abroad, especially from the USA. At the end of the war Britain owed the Americans about £1,000 million. Thus the true costs of the war had not yet been paid, and they would have to be borne by the postwar taxpayer.

The government also had to concern itself with other, more general, aspects of the economy. The submarine warfare in the Atlantic meant that imported goods, including food, were often in short supply, and so the government had to encourage the maximum production of home-grown food. It also had to take account of grievances over the cost of living. The war years were years of inflation. Food prices rose by ten per cent in the first month of war, occasioning hardship among the public, and the cost of living index (a general guide to British prices) rose steadily thereafter (see the table below). Prices had roughly doubled by 1918. Could wages keep pace with this inflation? Here was one significant problem for industrial relations, and there were others too. How would the trade unions react to the unprecedented changes of these years, and in particular to the admission of women to do 'men's work' in industry?

Wage and Price Levels		
	Prices	**Wages**
1914	100	100
1916	146	121
1918	203	195

2 Industrial Relations During the War

KEY ISSUES What degree of collaboration was achieved between government and unions during the war? Why did 'unofficial' strikes occur?

a) Collaboration

British trade unions reacted patriotically when the war began. The TUC called for an 'industrial truce' and urged that existing strikes be settled quickly. The number of working days lost in strikes in December 1914 totalled only three per cent of those lost in the last month of peace. Many unions even acted as recruiting agencies for the army. Union leaders recognised that the war could not be won unless their members rallied to the common cause, a fact of which the government was equally aware. There were therefore attempts to take the unions into partnership with government. It has been said that in 1914 British labour 'came of age' in that its position as a vital element in the economy was officially recognised. Labour and capital were seen to be equally important, and the government formed a 'triangular collaboration' with both.

Trade union leaders were given vital war work to do. Places were found in government for several of them, while the leader of the Labour Party, Arthur Henderson, soon became a member of the War Cabinet. In 1915 Lloyd George hammered out an important agreement with the unions. In March he invited union leaders to a three-day conference at the Treasury. The Labour newspaper, the *Daily Herald*, commented with some trepidation that 'the trade union lamb had lain down with the capitalist lion'.

The result was the 'Treasury Agreement', which specified that unions involved in vital war work would not strike: instead, if a compromise could not be reached by two sides in a dispute, an impartial tribunal would arrange arbitration. The unions also agreed to suspend traditional ('restrictive') working practices (such as specifying that only certain skilled men should undertake particular tasks) since these would tend to limit output. In return they were promised that the old arrangements would be resumed after the war and that the profits of firms benefiting from the agreement would be limited to 20 per cent above their 1914 levels. If profits exceeded this level, an excess profits tax of 100 per cent would be levied.

This was only a voluntary agreement, but in July 1915 it was followed by the Munitions of War Act. This went further, in that it was legally binding, and although it only applied at first to munitions workers, it could be extended to cover any other group. The Act banned strikes by workers and 'lockouts' by employers, made the restriction of output an offence (so that normal working practices and hours of employment could be changed), and put some safety regulations into abeyance. It also became illegal for workers in key production posts to switch jobs without permission: they would first have to obtain a 'leaving certificate'. This procedure was designed to prevent the loss of valuable production and to stop employers 'poaching' skilled workers from one another.

Some workers objected to these arrangements. They believed that since trade unions were no longer putting pressure on employers for higher wages and better conditions of service, they were no longer fulfilling their proper functions. Complaints were especially voluble against union acceptance of 'dilution' in 1915. Many trade unionists in skilled and vital jobs had volunteered to join the army, and since skilled craftsmen were not available to take their places, and it would take too long to train apprentices, trade union leaders accepted that it was necessary to replace them with unskilled workers, including women. Thus the job of the skilled worker was 'diluted' by being broken up into a series of simpler tasks which the unskilled could perform. Union officials even supervised the process of dilution and made sure it worked effectively. In this way, the unions were contributing significantly to the war effort. But to critics, the unions were not so much partners of the government as their lackeys.

b) Alternative Voices

How should the unions react to the war? Lloyd George had no doubt where their duty lay. While British soldiers were giving their lives,

British workers had a duty to rally to the cause. In a speech in February 1915 he said:

1   Much as I should like to talk about the need for more men, that is not the point of my special appeal today. We stand more in need of equipment that we do of men. This is an engineers' war, and it will be won or lost owing to the efforts or shortcomings of engineers ... We need
5   men, but we need arms more than men, and delay in producing them is full of peril for this country ... There are all sorts of regulations for restricting output. There are reasons why they have been built up ... The workmen had to fight for them for their own protection, but in a period of war there is a suspension of ordinary law. Output is every-
10   thing in this war.
      Most of our workmen are putting every ounce of strength into this urgent work for their country, loyally and patriotically. But that is not true of all. There are some, I am sorry to say, who shirk their duty in this great emergency. I hear of workmen in armaments works who
15   refuse to work a full week's work for the nation's needs ... They are a minority. The vast majority belong to a class we can depend upon. The others are in a minority. But, you must remember, a small minority of workmen can throw a whole works out of gear. What is the reason? Sometimes it is one thing, sometimes it is another, but let us be per-
20   fectly candid. It is mostly the lure of the drink ... Drink is doing us more damage in the war than all the German submarines put together.

Afterwards Lloyd George restricted the hours pubs could open and arranged that the alcohol content of drinks should be lowered, producing a marked fall in the incidence of drunkenness.

Many workers saw the need to accept sacrifices for the common effort. Yet there were alternative voices. One was that of a miners' leader, A.J. Cook, who had been an effective Baptist preacher in his earlier years and who had been much influenced by syndicalism. In April 1916 he urged miners to oppose collaboration with the capitalist enemy:

1   Daily I see signs amongst the working class with whom I move and work of a mighty awakening. The chloroforming pill of patriotism is failing in its power to drug the mind and consciousness of the worker. He is beginning to shudder at his stupidity in allowing himself to become a
5   party to such a catastrophe as we see today. The chains of slavery are being welded tighter upon us than ever. The ruling classes are over-reaching themselves in their hurry to enslave us ... Economic conditions are forcing the workers to think; the scales are falling from their eyes. Men are wanted to give a lead. Comrades, I appeal to you to
10   rouse your union to protect the liberties of its members. An industrial truce was entered into by our leaders behind our backs which has opened the way for any encroachment upon our rights and liberties. Away with the industrial truce. We must not stand by and allow the workers to be exploited and our liberties taken away.

Militant trade unionists were willing to challenge not only the government but also their own moderate leaders during the war. The unions were in a very strong position because there was full employment. Union membership increased from about 4 million at the start of the war to 6 million at its close. Trade union leaders could have used this strength to extract concessions from employers and the government, but instead they accepted the need for sacrifice. Yet could they take their membership with them? As the war dragged on and as the cost of living rose, a great strain was put on their loyalty.

c) Conflict

In many ways, trade unionists made important gains during the war. The fact that government controlled so much of industry led to national, as opposed to local, wage agreements. The miners finally achieved their aim of national wage rates. Furthermore, the length of the average working week fell from 55 to 45 hours. In some industries much better conditions of service came about. In the docks, for instance, the 'decasualisation' of labour began. Before the war, men were selected for employment on a daily basis, as ships needed to be loaded or unloaded, and so did not earn regular wages. But during the wartime shortage of labour, the dockers were given regular contracts of employment. A welfare department in the Ministry of Munitions also helped to bring about much improved conditions of work, so that almost 1,000 works canteens were built. It was coming to be realised that welfare was a vital factor in producing efficiency.

The main factor promoting tension was inflation. Wage rates rose during the war, so that by 1918 real wages stood, on average, only a few per cent below their 1914 levels (see table on page 40). Indeed these wage rates do not take account of overtime payments, so that not all workers were marginally worse off by the end of the war and some were much better off. Yet an annual inflation rate of about 25 per cent undoubtedly exacerbated industrial tensions, and around the middle of the war wages seemed to lag significantly behind prices. Furthermore there were some sectors of the economy whose wages lagged behind prices for the duration. In fact the First World War, which saw so much harmony in industrial relations, also saw significant strife.

Strikes had been outlawed in 1915, and over the next years the government set up machinery to arbitrate between workers and employers. It was arranged that in each industry there would be a joint council of employers and union representatives at national, district and works levels. But still strikes occurred. In fact only two weeks after industrial action was forbidden, 200,000 miners went on an unofficial strike in South Wales. It was impossible to arrest so many law-breakers, so the government put pressure on the mine owners to grant the men's demands for wage increases. The following year the government decided to take control of the mines itself in order to prevent further trouble.

The other main area of industrial conflict in the early years of the war was on Clydeside, in the shipyards of Glasgow. Here many craftsmen were angered by the acceptance of dilution by their union, the Amalgamated Society of Engineers, and their grievances were taken up by those who, before the war, had been influenced by syndicalism. The war had been a tremendous blow for those who wished to see working-class solidarity against the capitalist oppressors, but it was not a final defeat. Alternative leaders stepped in to perform the duties which the official union leaders now seemed unwilling to undertake. These were shop stewards, men appointed before the war to represent union members in individual workshops. Now they claimed to speak for all the men, of every union or of none. They were the most radical – and perhaps revolutionary – figures on the left during the war.

Glasgow's shop stewards opposed both the Treasury Agreement and the Munitions Act. They arranged several unofficial strikes in 1915, and when at the end of the year a victory was won – and steeply rising rents were pegged to their 1914 level – their prestige was high. They set up the Clyde Workers' Committee. Lloyd George himself decided to visit the Clyde to appeal for unity in December 1915. Everything was carefully stage-managed: there were workers in khaki uniform, a choir sang patriotic songs, the Union Jack was proudly displayed, and Labour's Arthur Henderson introduced him – but all to no avail. Disrespectful cries of 'Get your hair cut' rang out, and soon Lloyd George was shouted down. He was told that the Munitions Act 'has the taint of slavery about it'.

The shop stewards opposed dilution on the Clyde, but the government imposed it nevertheless, despite a series of strikes in 1916. Seven shop stewards were arrested and imprisoned for sedition, while others were deported to other areas of Scotland. Government spokesmen claimed that a major attempt to sabotage the war effort had been averted. The movement had certainly been dealt a major blow. Defeat on the Clyde was followed by an attempt to create a nationwide shop stewards' movement, but without much success. Perhaps the shop stewards' fundamental weakness was that, whereas they themselves were radicals (and some even revolutionaries), their main support came from a group of very conservative craftsmen, whose central concern was to preserve traditional practices and their own high rates of pay. Such men were willing to fight a rearguard action to maintain their own privileges, but fundamentally there was little in common between their outlook and that of the shop stewards.

The Clyde was relatively quiet in 1917 and 1918, but not so British industry as a whole. In 1917, a rash of strikes threatened the whole war effort. Over 5.6 million working days were lost in 1917 (more than in the previous two years combined), and roughly the same number in 1918. In May 1917 there were engineers' strikes in Coventry, Manchester, Sheffield and elsewhere. An enquiry revealed many of the causes of the trouble. People were angry about high food prices, high rents and war profiteering. The excess profits tax was being widely avoided. There was also a high degree of overcrowding, as very few houses were built during the war, and conscription was proving very unpopular. It was also found that many workers believed that their trade union officials 'are no longer to be relied on'.

There were, in fact, unmistakable signs that the population was war-weary, drawing from one historian the comment that 'civilian willpower was near to breaking point'. The government denounced the strikes as 'unpatriotic activity' – a charge reiterated in a *Punch* cartoon (see page 46) – and some ministers wished to declare martial law and conscript the strikers. But the Prime Minister decided that the only real answer was to grant pay rises so that real wages could return to their accustomed levels. The government also abandoned the 'leaving certificate', which was proving unpopular.

The strikes were, on the whole, not a sign of revolutionary activity. Indeed one might be surprised that industrial unrest was not more pronounced towards the end of the war. Strikes arose mainly because the government could neither stop inflation nor devise a means of adjusting national wages in line with it. At the same time, calls for workers to show patriotism had begun to wear thin. Lloyd George commented in Cabinet that, at bottom, workers' grievances were 'genuine and legitimate', though adding that there was a real danger that these would be 'exploited by violent anarchists'.

Industrial unrest worried the government enormously in 1917 and 1918. The Bolshevik revolution in Russia seemed to give a fillip to revolutionary groups in Britain, and it was tempting to believe that deep-seated plots lay behind the wave of strikes of this period. There were rumours of a possible general strike, and a workers' soviet was set up in Glasgow, before its leader was sentenced to five years' imprisonment with hard labour. Nevertheless, despite these fears and isolated incidents, enough was done by the end of the war to remove grievances and so to blunt the edge of militancy.

3 The Changing Roles of Women

> **KEY ISSUE** In what ways did the war affect women's position in society?

a) Prewar

To many men in Edwardian Britain, the world was being turned upside down. In particular they objected to new-fangled notions about women. The traditional view, of which they approved, was that women and men were fitted by nature to perform very different tasks. Evidently men had, in the course of evolution, developed their intelligence; women, however, had woefully neglected this faculty and focused instead on physical beauty, with the prime purpose of securing a mate and perpetuating the species. A woman's body was essentially geared to reproduction and the nurture of their offspring – hence the lighter brain of the female and her incapacity to think logically. 'The true destiny of a woman,' wrote Thomas Carlyle in 1871, voicing what seemed a self-evident truth, 'is to wed a man she can love and esteem'. The natural woman was gentle and self-effacing, and her

THE TRAITOR.

Punch cartoon, 'The Traitor', 2 October 1918

true role in life was to care for her children, her home and her husband. Her place was in the home.

Women were not inferior to men, so the message ran, they simply had different natures which demanded 'separate spheres' for their activity. Men and women complemented each other. 'Man for the field, woman for the hearth', as Tennyson put it; 'Man to command and woman to obey'. It seemed (especially to men!) the perfect division of labour. Yet by the early years of the twentieth century this ideology was wearing very thin.

First of all, this essentially Victorian interpretation of women was always based on class hypocrisy. While middle-class women were seen as 'angels of the home', 600,000 working-class women, mainly single, worked in textile factories in the north of England around 1911. (At the same time, there were 1.6 million female domestic servants, depriving upper- and middle-class women of their home-making rights.) Secondly, there were more women than men – and by the end of the nineteenth century one in four women would never marry – and no one knew quite what to do with the 'surplus'. Most important of all, although many women accepted the male propaganda that their essential function in life was to 'service' men, a large minority did not. Some married women even wanted to break the taboo on their taking paid employment. Of course an uncomfortably large number of women were, and always had been, dominant characters. In Salford, for instance, Roberts noted that 'In our communities, the matriarchs stood guardians'. Now women were becoming nurses and teachers, thereby extending the traditional image of woman as a carer. What was worse, individual women were making names for themselves as explorers (for instance, Mary Kingsley), as doctors (including Elizabeth Garrett Anderson) and in the other professions. Although girls on average received far less, and far inferior, education than boys, there were growing numbers of female graduates by the end of the century.

Women were challenging the stereotypes by which a male-dominated society sought to control them. They wanted equality, and the touchstone of this was the vote. Some women were eligible to vote in local elections from 1869, and in the following decade were themselves elected to positions in local administration. But no woman could vote in national elections. The Reform Acts of 1832, 1867 and 1884 progressively extended the franchise to men, so that eventually two in every three men could vote, even some who were illiterate. Yet no woman, even the most intelligent and well educated, had the right to do so.

In response the National Union of Women's Suffrage Societies was founded in 1897 by Millicent Fawcett, and this was followed in 1903 by the Women's Social and Political Union, under the leadership of Emmeline Pankhurst. Over the next years many male politicians, from across the political spectrum, were converted to the cause of female suffrage, and yet no legislation was enacted. Part of the trouble was a lack of consensus on the form that a new Reform Bill should take. If women received the vote on the same terms as men, that would probably benefit the Conservatives – and so the Liberals, in power from 1905, favoured a more thoroughgoing measure of reform, which would also enfranchise more working-class men. But the political will for this was lacking.

The 'suffraggists' of Mrs Fawcett were moderate and law-abiding in their tactics. Not so the more militant 'suffragettes' of Mrs Pankhurst, who disrupted the Liberals' election campaign in 1905 and in the following years escalated their tactics to include vandalism, arson and physical attacks on ministers. Many courted arrest and then went on hunger strike. They won great publicity, and 'votes for women' was seldom off the political agenda; but their violence probably alienated many potential supporters and convinced many reactionary men that women were indeed unfitted for the vote. The *Manchester Guardian*, for instance, attacked the 'diseased emotionalism' of the suffragettes.

With the outbreak of war in August 1914, however, the suffragettes suspended their campaigns and decided instead to back the government. Emmeline Pankhurst had long harboured suspicions about German militarism, and now she not only renamed her journal *Suffragette* with the patriotic title *Britannia* but she undertook recruitment work for the government.

b) War-time

Massive recruitment for the armed forces meant a shortage of domestic workers, and now the all-male government had few qualms about recruiting women. About 750,000 women took jobs in manufacturing, and especially munitions production. For instance, while Woolwich Arsenal had employed 125 women in 1914, it had 28,000 female employees in 1918. Another 750,000 women took on clerical, transport and other work. No longer did it signify whether a woman worker was married or not, and indeed around 40 per cent of female workers during the war were married. Furthermore, some large firms set up nurseries for children, convincing many – men and women – that the roles of wage-earner and mother were not irreconcilable. Women laboured on the surface of coal mines, they became porters and bus-conductors and did other 'unfeminine' jobs. Some of their work was unskilled, but they also took over many skilled jobs, which were now 'diluted' into simpler tasks. One skilled engineering job, for instance, was broken down into 22 separate tasks performed by 22 women.

In addition around 100,000 women joined the Women's Auxiliary Army Corps, the Women's Royal Naval Service, the Women's Royal Air Force and the Land Army. They did no actual fighting, serving largely as drivers, telephonists, messengers, cooks and storekeepers; but women in the Voluntary Aid Detachments nursed the sick and wounded at home and at the front.

The number of paid women workers grew by 1.5 million during the war and they pursued a much greater range of occupations than ever before: this constituted a highly significant change in employment patterns and in the position of women in British society. A blow was being dealt to the Victorian belief that a woman's place was in the home and that women's work outside the home should be restricted to traditional 'caring' roles.

On the other hand, old habits of mind persisted. Many women suffered sexual harassment from male colleagues; the breaking-down of skilled work into so many simpler tasks often underestimated women's capacities; and women received, on average, only two-thirds of men's wages. Admittedly, many women now rejected the old, prewar image of themselves: they wanted to be 'breadwinners not brides'. But would they be given the opportunity once the war was over? How long-lasting were the changes in a woman's lot that the war had brought about?

4 Conclusion: Effects of the War

> **KEY ISSUE** How significant were the overall effects brought about by the war which ended on 11 November 1918?

a) Government

The powers of the state had grown enormously. A form of 'war socialism' had been introduced. Never before had any British government had such power over its citizens: it told them where to work, what to eat (with its rationing policies) and even what to think (via extensive propaganda). New ministries were set up, and at the end of the war several of these – Pensions, Health and Labour – became permanent institutions of the state. There had been an important extension of social policy during the war, and by 1918 the government was formulating extensive plans for the provision of new housing, better education and an extension of unemployment insurance.

Of course many war-time developments would probably have occurred anyway. It is extremely likely, for instance, that Lloyd George would, sooner or later, have become prime minister. Greater state intervention built upon the abandonment of *laissez-faire* by the

'New Liberals' before 1914. It is also true that shortly after the war the government retreated from its vision of a 'land fit for heroes' (see page 116). Nevertheless, taxation and social spending did not return to their prewar levels. The war had speeded up processes already under way and had created a new context in which politicians operated, not least because in 1918 the electorate was virtually trebled, from 7.5 million men to 21 million adults. The vote was extended to all men over the age of 21, on the grounds that those who had worked and fought for their country were entitled to choose its government. In addition, women over 30 received the vote as well (see page 76)

b) The Economy

The war had produced major economic changes. British industry had been to a large extent transformed by the mobilisation of millions of soldiers and by an unprecedented switch to war production.

On the positive side, the economy had shown a new productive capacity. One historian has commented that 'The stimulus of war ... infused a fresh spirit of enterprise into British industry'. Total output had fallen slightly, because of the smaller workforce, but productivity had definitely increased. There had been much state-sponsored modernisation, including a greater standardisation of engineering products. Electric power was used more than ever before, especially in the munitions factories, and the aircraft industry had developed significantly. The removal of so many skilled workers from industry, which had initially seemed to threaten economic collapse, had in fact stimulated much needed mechanisation. The efficiency of agriculture had also increased, with the widespread introduction of the tractor.

Such changes might have occurred even without the war, though at a slower pace. But the same cannot be said of other war-time developments, most notably the casualties incurred. About 750,000 men had perished in the conflict (nine per cent of all men under 45 years of age), and twice that number had been very badly wounded. A productive section of the workforce had been lost. Soon 3.5 million people, including widows and orphans, were receiving some form of war pension or allowance; and as late as 1928 there were 48 mental hospitals helping over 60,000 victims of 'shell shock'. In addition, Britain still had to pay the financial costs of the war. Massive amounts of money had been borrowed and would have to be repaid, while British loans to Russia were repudiated by the new Soviet government. In fact the National Debt had increased twelvefold by 1919. In addition, valuable overseas assets had been sold. Even before the war, Britain had imported goods of greater value than those it exported, and now that overseas investments had diminished the so-called 'invisible exports' would not be so lucrative. In addition, valuable overseas markets had been lost. Could Britain win back its former customers?

There was another major problem too. The prewar economy had been dangerously dependent on the old 'staple industries', but high wartime demand for iron and steel, coal and textiles had resulted in further massive investment in them. Unless these products continued to sell in vast amounts, which was highly unlikely, there would be unemployment ahead. Would the war accentuate Britain's relative economic decline?

c) Industrial Relations

There were further unanswered questions in the field of industrial relations. Would the partnership between government and trade unions be maintained after the war? There had already been signs in 1917–18 that it was seriously under threat. Were the strikes of this period a sign of a fundamental antagonism between capital and labour that might even produce some sort of revolution? This was a real fear.

It was also uncertain whether official trade union leadership would be able to guide working-class discontent into constructive and constitutional channels or whether the shop stewards' movement or other radicals would take control. Would normal working practices be resumed, as the government had promised, or would employers seek to perpetuate wartime arrangements? If the latter, then the shop stewards might well find increasing support. If the former, how would women react on being forced to leave industry?

On average, by the end of the war rates of pay had virtually returned to their prewar levels, in real terms. But there were significant variations between different groups of workers. Pay differentials had been eroded. Before the war, a skilled worker might earn two or three times as much as an unskilled colleague. Now this inequality had diminished, partly because wartime pay rises were often flat-rate increases (set amounts) rather than percentages and partly because unskilled workers were put on 'piecework', a system where pay depended on output. As a result, many unskilled workers, with overtime, were taking home much more money than ever before, some more than skilled workers. Would the craftsmen now attempt to return to their privileged position? And would workers as a whole, having shown restraint during the war, seek large increases now that the war was over? And what of those employees, such as teachers, whose pay had failed to keep up with price rises? Would they now take to strike action?

By the end of the war joint councils had been set up for several industries, composed of representatives of workers and employers. It was hoped that these would promote industrial peace by settling wages and conditions of service by negotiation and compromise. Could these herald for peacetime a new and more constructive method of settling industrial problems than the old way of confrontation and strikes? No one could yet be certain.

d) Women

The war had been a very significant period for British women. They entered the world of work in greater numbers than ever before and gave the lie to the notion they were unfitted for activity outside the home. They also received the vote, billboards proclaiming in 1918 that 'The Nation Thanks the Women'. This might seem a supreme example of the 'Military Participation Ratio' – women's high-profile involvement in the war produced a corresponding degree of change.

Yet clearly this theory is inadequate. (Theories like the Military Participation Ratio are rarely adequate to explain the complexity of human history, which contains too many variables to be reduced to simple formulae.) First, only women over 30 received the vote; and yet women in their twenties had done much to earn the nation's gratitude. Secondly, there were a variety of reasons for women's enfranchisement, one factor being fear of renewed suffragette activity. Probably a majority of male MPs in 1914 had favoured votes for women, and enfranchisement would have occurred sooner or later even without the war.

We also have to recognise that the economic gains for women from the war were short-lived. Most women lost their jobs to returning soldiers (see page 75). In 1921 women constituted 29 per cent of the workforce, exactly the same total as in 1911. The First World War did have its effects, especially on the psychology of the women who participated in it; but it was not a revolutionary turning point.

Summary diagram
The First World War

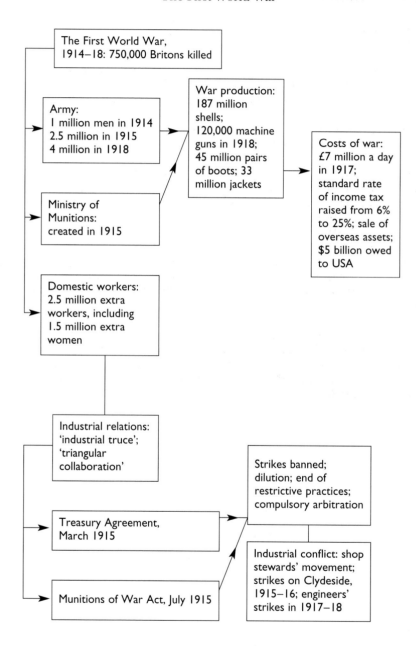

Working on Chapter 3

You need to compile a detailed summary of this chapter. The headings, Key Issues and sub headings should help you to organise the material efficiently. As in the previous chapter, you should try to expand the final section ('Conclusion') by attempting to formulate your own judgements about the significance of the war years. Bear in mind that 'significance' depends on future developments – so return to this section after you have read the rest of the book.

Answering structured and essay questions on Chapter 3

Consider the following structured question:

a) By what means did British governments attempt to foster good industrial relations between 1914 and 1918? (*15 marks*)
b) Account for the strikes that occurred during the First World War. (*15 marks*)
c) How well did governments manage industrial relations during the war? (*15 marks*)

There are equal marks for each part of the question, and so you might well wish to spend equal time on each. But don't think you have to write the same amount on each. The first two parts are basically factual, and you should include a good deal of information. The third part, however, requires much more careful thought and evaluation. You need to present an argument, and in so doing you will refer or allude to information given in the first two parts without repeating it. Hence a good answer to c) could be relatively short. (Think of it as the concluding paragraph of an A2 essay – see page 34.)

Essay questions can centre on industrial relations, either in 1914–18 or bracketed in a wider timescale, or on wartime women. But perhaps the most popular question on the war years looks at the degree to which the war produced economic change in Britain. A typical title is:

1. To what extent did the First World War lead to economic change on the Home Front between 1914 and 1918?

It is worth spending some time trying to work out an overall argument in answer to this question. This might then form the basis of a final paragraph. How might you proceed? Think in terms of a) the degree of overall ('quantitative') economic change, and then b) the types of particular change ('qualitative'). Perhaps try a 'brain-storming' session. Which particular groups of workers might you focus on? Do you think it will be relevant to stress the degree to which Britain's international trading position was affected, or does the 'Home Front' preclude this aspect? Make sure that the form of words you choose answers the question directly: since it asks 'to what extent' you must conclude by specifying the extent as precisely as possible.

Source-based questions on Chapter 3

1. The Home Front
Read the extracts from speeches by Lloyd George and A.J. Cook on page 42 and study the cartoon on page 46. Answer the following questions:

a) With what justification did Lloyd George say that 'we need arms more than men' (page 42 line 5)? (*4 marks*)
b) How much appreciation did Lloyd George show of the difficulties faced by trade unionists and workers generally? Explain your answer. (*5 marks*)
c) What did Cook mean by 'the chloroforming pill of patriotism' (page 42 line 2)? (*2 marks*)
d) To what was Cook referring when he said that 'our rights and liberties' (page 42 line 12) were being encroached upon? (*3 marks*)
e) Which of the two speeches do you think would have had more appeal to British workers in 1915–16? Explain your answer. (*6 marks*)
f) How does the depiction of the two men in the cartoon help to convey its central message? (*6 marks*)
g) Use your knowledge to estimate how far these sources explain why strikes occurred during the war and what was done to combat them. (*14 marks*)

4 The Interwar Years: Britain in Decline?

POINTS TO CONSIDER

In this chapter you have to consider the British economy between the wars. How did different sectors perform over this period, and what overall trends are visible? Try to see both positive and negative features and reach a balanced overall verdict, one that is neither 'optimistic' nor 'pessimistic'. The economy exhibited wide variations, and the same is true of British society, where wealth and poverty coexisted. The 1930s were marked by high unemployment and extensive poverty, and social surveys allow us to know more about poverty in this period than ever before. But does this mean that Britain was in decline, or was poverty less extensive and severe than in previous periods?

KEY DATES

1919	Economic boom; Restoration of Pre-war Practices Act.
1920	Continued boom.
1921	Economic slump.
1926	Creation of the Central Electricity Board and of ICI.
1929 Oct	Wall Street Crash heralds depression.
1931	3 million unemployed (22% of insured workforce); unemployment and other benefits cut by 10%.
1936	Rowntree's second survey of York.
1938	Unemployment rose to 2 million.
1939 Sept	Second World War began.

1 Introduction

> **KEY ISSUE** Why is it so difficult to measure economic performance?

How did the British economy perform between 1918 and 1939? This seems like a straightforward question, involving 'fact' rather than 'interpretation'. Surely statistics will provide an objective answer. Yet this issue has resulted in considerable controversy. The interwar years have been seen by many historians as a period of rapid and irrevocable economic decline when the old Victorian economy 'crashed in ruins', resulting in mass unemployment. But others have depicted the two decades between the wars as a time of successful economic modernisation and of high productivity.

A related question concerns British society. Was this a period of social decline, i.e. of increased poverty, deprivation and ill health for the mass of British people – of 'Britain on the breadline'? Or, on the contrary, was it a period when living standards rose and affluence dawned? Clearly social trends will reflect economic performance.

The first essential is to realise the complexity of the seemingly simple question 'How did the economy perform between 1918 and 1939?' Most historians would respond to this question with a whole series of their own:

- Which sector(s) of the economy are we concerned with? The British economy was not monolithic (a single unit). Clearly we must look at as many different sectors of the economy as possible – at least at the old staple industries and at the new industries, like cars, electrical goods, and so on. But we should also look at the so-called 'service' industries, like transport, retailing, administration and entertainment, and the financial services sector, including Britain's overseas investments and 'invisible exports'. Nor should we forget agriculture, for if man cannot live by bread alone, it is certain that human beings cannot exist without food. We should also be aware of the regional variations of the British economy. Parts of the country fared very differently from each other because different sectors of the economy were sited in them.
- How do we measure economic 'performance'? Should we take account, above all else, of output – of the amounts being produced by industry and agriculture? If so, then gross domestic product (GDP) will be our main yardstick. But perhaps productivity (output per worker) is a better measure since it tends to reflect technological innovation and the 'modernisation' of industry. Should we emphasise the level of profits earned by industrialists? Or perhaps we should measure economic performance by the benefits that accrued more widely, in other words by the standard of living of the workers and their families – in which case levels of employment – and of unemployment – must be taken into account? The (uncomfortable) fact is that there are no universally accepted standards by which to measure economic performance.
- It is also important to see the British economy between 1918 and 1939 in perspective. This involves comparing its performance with earlier and later periods in British history (thus enabling us to see 'absolute' decline or progress) and with foreign economies (thus enabling us to see 'relative' decline or progress). An alternative is to try to compare actual economic performance with the optimum that could have been achieved (an interesting approach but also an extremely difficult one).
- Which particular time should we focus on? Economic activity moves in cycles. Economic historians often talk of the 'trade cycle' or 'business cycle'. These terms perhaps imply a greater regularity in the pattern of economic activity than is ever really the case, but they are useful nevertheless. Economic activity has 'troughs' and 'peaks' and thus can best be represented diagrammatically by curves rather than straight lines. Thus

there was no 'typical' year between the wars, and there was no single pattern of decline or progress. Much therefore depends on precisely which part of the period we are considering.

Clearly there are difficulties in examining British economic performance, especially when we add the perennial question of the reliability of statistics to the above problems. Statistical data are probably more reliable for the interwar years than for any previous period, but even so we must make allowances for inadequacies and margins of error and for the variety of ways in which statistics may be interpreted.

Nevertheless, while being cautious, we should not be defeatist. We do in fact know a tremendous amount about the interwar economy. For instance, most historians are agreed on the broad pattern of the trade cycle, with a peak just after the war giving way to a trough in 1921–2 and then a recovery until the worst depression of the period in 1929–32. Recovery then followed, before another minor downturn at the end of 1937. In 1938–9 rearmament produced further economic growth. It is convenient to examine the economy within this broad chronological framework.

2 1918–22: the Postwar Years

> **KEY ISSUES** What is meant by 'cyclical' and 'structural' unemployment? Why did the postwar bubble of prosperity burst?

a) Boom

There was great optimism at the end of 1918. People called for a better and more fulfilling life for those who had survived the war; and Lloyd George, the Prime Minister, won a general election on the slogans 'a land fit for heroes' and 'homes for heroes'. Such promises were immensely popular. The hard question was whether the economy could possibly allow their realisation.

The war had contradictory effects on the British economy (see page 50). Many lives had been lost, much destruction had occurred and, moreover, vast debts had been accumulated. On the other hand, the war had stimulated a large amount of modernisation. Were the overall results positive or negative? For a time it seemed that they were positive, as a boom occurred in 1919 and 1920. Civilian industries were restocking and pent-up consumer demand was great: British industry therefore expanded to satisfy this high level of demand. Similarly, export industries did well and it seemed that Britain would play a leading role in Europe's recovery from the devastation of war. All seemed set fair. There was little unemployment, so that in 1920 only 2.6 per cent of insured workers were without a job. Profits and wages were rising, industrial production grew by about 20 per cent within two years of the end of the fighting, and there was also a rise on the stock market.

b) Bust

It was all too good to last, and in the winter of 1920–21 the bubble burst. Production soon exceeded consumption and a brief but deep depression began. In December 1920 unemployment more than doubled, and in June 1921 it stood at over two million (18 per cent of the insured workforce). Industrial production slumped alarmingly: figures for 1921 were slightly lower than those for 1918, while exports declined by half during the year. Prices fell as sharply as they had risen, so that inflation was replaced by deflation – in other words, the prices of goods fell rather than rose, so that money was worth more not less. In fact the interwar period was henceforth characterised by deflation.

The trouble stemmed in part from a world economic slump, but it was also due to peculiar British circumstances. During the war the urgent demand for the products of Britain's staple industries led to massive investment, and this continued even after the war. But by 1921 it was clear that there had been substantial over-investment and that the boom had been fuelled by what the *Economist* called a 'craze for speculation'. Many companies had expanded rapidly but unwisely, borrowing large sums against the expectation of future profits that failed to materialise. The world no longer needed British staple goods in anything like the same quantities.

Britain's capacity to produce steel had expanded by 50 per cent during the war, but in the postwar period neither the domestic economy nor export orders could absorb such quantities. Too many other countries were producing their own steel. It was the same with shipping. During the war there had been an insatiable demand, and in 1920 Britain built 2 million tons of shipping. But merchant vessels were no longer being sunk by enemy submarines, and soon shipbuilding had to be scaled back to little more than 0.5 million tons a year. Nor was British coal such a valuable commodity: not only were other countries now supplying coal to the world market, but gas and electricity had emerged as rival industrial fuels and ships had begun to be powered by oil. In addition, hydro-electric power was beginning to be exploited in Scotland and Wales. The textile industry suffered as well: overseas markets had been lost during the war to the Japanese and other competitors, and they could not be won back.

Even before the war the old staple industries had been relatively depressed. Clearly Britain needed to diversify in order to regain a competitive economic edge. Then the war had produced significant over-capacity in these industries. As a result, in areas of the country like South Wales, the North-West and North-East of England and

Clydeside in Scotland, as well as Northern Ireland, there were soon massive lay-offs of workers. What economists term 'structural unemployment' had come to Britain: this was unemployment resulting from the structure of the British economy and not merely from a trough in the trade cycle. Mass unemployment in 1921–2 coincided with the downturn of the cycle, but when the recession ended a million men – including many miners, steel workers, shipbuilders and textile workers – were still without a job. While 'cyclical' unemployment by its very nature tends to be short-term, 'structural' unemployment is likely to last much longer. Many workers made redundant in 1921 were to remain unemployed throughout the interwar period. There were at least a million people unemployed in Britain – the 'intractable ten per cent' of the insured workforce – from 1921 until 1940.

3 The Recovery of 1923–9

> **KEY ISSUE** Why have historians interpreted economic performance in these years in contrasting ways?

a) The Pessimistic View

According to several historians, the existence of mass unemployment was the most significant fact about the whole interwar economy. Given that over a million workers were continuously unemployed, it followed that the British economy was not performing near full (or optimum) capacity. The employment record of 1923–9 looks especially poor when compared with other countries. In the United States the post-war boom lasted until 1929: these were the so-called 'Roaring Twenties'. In France, too, 1923–9 was a time of economic expansion and high employment, and the French economy had suffered even more from the war than Britain's. By 1928 there was full employment in France: fewer than 600 people were claiming unemployment benefit and several million immigrant workers had found jobs in French industry.

There is other evidence that the British economy performed badly in this period. In 1920–9 the value of Britain's imports exceeded that of her exports: there was a sizable 'current account' deficit. Britain's trading position was significantly weaker than before the war. In fact there was an overall balance of payments surplus because of Britain's 'invisible exports', but these were no longer nearly as lucrative as before 1914. The war, and then war debts and reparations, had helped to destroy the old international financial order which Britain had dominated. The City of London could not win back its former position as financial capital of the world and, because some foreign investments had been sold, profits from overseas investment income were lower than before 1914. The United States was now lending more money than Britain, and the dollar replaced the pound as the dominant international currency. As a result, Britain had a smaller overall balance of payments surplus than prewar.

A smaller proportion of GDP was also invested domestically than before the war, a worrying fact given that the new industries tended to be capital-intensive (relying on expensive machinery rather than on a large labour force). Put simply, it seems that Britain's relative decline continued. During the 1920s Britain's share of world exports fell from just under 18 per cent to just under 11 per cent. Statistical indices show that while in 1929 British manufacturing output equalled that of 1913, US production had risen by 80 per cent, France's by 40 per cent and Japan's by 200 per cent. British economic decline in these years was, it has been said, 'a palpable fact'.

b) The Optimistic View

Yet there is a school of historians which emphasises the positive aspects of the mid-1920s. There was, according to one historian, 'a sort of boom' in this period. The City of London, for instance, may not have been as dominant in world finance as hitherto, but even so it continued to earn high profits and to put the balance of payments in the black. These historians, while admitting the high levels of unemployment, point out that despite under-utilised manpower the economy enjoyed considerable success. They estimate, for instance, that between 1920 and 1929 industrial production grew by an average of 2.8 per cent a year, double the rate of growth of the pre-war years (1899–1913).

Indices of productivity are among the hardest to calculate. This is because it is so difficult to make allowances for the changing number of hours that people worked and also for the quality of the goods produced. Increases in productivity can also be misleading, since so much depends on the starting point: an inefficient economy can make startling increases in productivity and still be less efficient than a rival economy, making much lower productivity increases but operating from a higher initial level. Nevertheless, according to the available data, the British economy achieved an excellent rate of productivity in the 1920s. Output per worker per hour expanded by an average of 3.8 per cent a year in this decade. Based on these figures, the British economy did better than most of its economic rivals.

No longer were the staple industries employing so many people, and no longer were they producing or exporting so much. But they enjoyed significant increases in productivity. In the mining industry productivity increased by a total of 18 per cent between 1924 and 1930, while in the iron and steel industry there were increases of 25 per cent. In addition, major strides were made in the new industries, as investment shifted to electrical engineering, motor vehicles, chemicals, new man-made fibres such as rayon (artificial silk), and to paper and printing. Imperial Chemical Industries (ICI) was founded in 1926. Such industries often adopted the most modern equipment and the most up-to-date production techniques, utilising the conveyor-belt system. This sector also experienced a large number of mergers of companies, which made for greater efficiency. For example, the number of car manufacturers fell by half in the 1920s, and over the same period output grew by a very healthy 6 per cent a year while the price of an average car fell by about one-third. Clearly, the overall figures which show that in 1929 Britain was producing only as much as in 1913 disguise the transformation of the economy that was beginning to take place.

One of the most important new factors producing growth in the 1920s was the Central Electricity Board, created in 1926. The Board gave an important impetus to the generation of electricity, so that a completely new network of power stations was built, and it also constructed a system of high-voltage transmission lines ('the national grid'). Not only did homes benefit – so that whereas in 1920 only one in 17 houses was wired for electricity, ten years later the figure had risen to one in three – but industry generally was profoundly affected. New electrically-powered industries were now set up away from coalfields, the traditional source of energy, and near to the largest consumer markets. A large-scale relocation of industry began, and the dominant sectors of the economy were soon sited in the Midlands and the South East. Furthermore, electricity produced a growth in consumer goods industries, as electrical appliances such as radios and vacuum cleaners became popular.

The 1920s have been called 'a watershed between the old industrial regime of the pre-1914 era and the new industrial economy of the post-1945 period'. This 'new' economy included a growing 'service' sector. Large retailing stores multiplied in the 1920s, so that Marks and Spencers, Boots, Woolworths and Sainsbury's all began, and the advertising industry became important. In the 1930s many of these developments continued apace, but in other respects a sharp break occurred in 1929.

4 The Great Depression, 1929–32

> **KEY ISSUE** What made the economic depression so acute in Britain?

a) Origins

In 1929 the most severe depression of modern times began. Its longer-term origins stemmed from the disruptive effects of the First

World War. More specifically it arose from speculation on the Wall Street stock market in the United States. A mania for speculation pushed stocks and shares to record heights, so that fortunes were made very rapidly. Many people bought shares on credit, hoping to pay for them and make a profit by quick re-sales. The problem was that the inflated prices of shares bore little relation to the fundamental value of the companies they were supposed to represent. When confidence dipped in October 1929 the stock market crashed: 24 October was 'Black Thursday'. A loss of confidence made people sell their shares and so prices fell, which produced further falls in confidence and still more sales and still lower prices. A 'vicious circle' was created. By the end of the month American investors had lost $40,000 million. The stock market only stabilised when 80 per cent of its value had been lost. But the problems did not end there. Over the next years, thousands of American banks went bankrupt, the demand for goods fell and unemployment rose to about 13 million in 1933.

The depression quickly reached the rest of the world. American bankers were no longer prepared to lend money abroad, while short-term US loans ('hot money') were recalled. Furthermore, American consumption fell, and as a result exports to the USA suffered badly. The lower demand for goods meant that their prices slumped. 'Primary products' (raw materials, as distinct from manufactured goods) were especially badly hit: producers tended to compensate for lower prices by exporting greater volumes, but the resulting glut on the world market only depressed prices still more. Almost everywhere unemployment increased as business confidence disappeared.

b) Effects on Britain

In Britain the value of exports virtually halved between 1929 and 1931, and there was a deficit on visible trade for which not even 'invisibles' could compensate. Over the same period unemployment mounted. The one million unemployed at the start of 1929 quickly doubled, and in 1931–2 almost three million people were out of work – about 22 per cent of the insured workforce. In addition, there were probably another 750,000 people unemployed who, for various reasons, did not appear on the registers. In total, around eight million people, including dependants, lived on the dole in the worst months of the depression. Rates of unemployment were as bad in Britain as in the United States or Germany. The British economy was in crisis. No banks collapsed, as they did in America and continental Europe, but in 1931 there was an overall balance of payments deficit of £100 million which provoked political crisis and led to the downfall of the second Labour government (see page 127).

Many Britons thought that this depression was not just a particularly acute trough in the trade cycle. Hardly anyone could foresee an end to it all, and pessimists believed that the whole capitalist system was breaking down.

5 Economic Recovery, 1932–9

> **KEY ISSUE** Why did different parts of the country experience such contrasting economic fortunes in this period?

Britain's economic performance between 1932 and 1939 has been the subject of extensive debate. As for the 1920s, there has been a divergence of opinion between the 'pessimists' (stressing high unemployment and the further decline of the old staple industries), and the 'optimists' (focusing on the growth of new consumer goods industries and high levels of productivity). The Thirties have been seen as a period of economic stagnation by some and of substantial economic progress by others. Not surprisingly, each of the two schools of thought has to a large extent concentrated on different aspects of these years, and many recent writers have tried to show that the two views are in fact complementary rather than contradictory. The 1930s are often seen now as 'a decade of contrasts', a period of paradox.

a) Levels of Unemployment

Unemployment totals give a useful indication of the severity of the depression and of recovery from it. The peak of the depression was reached in the early months of 1932, when almost three million people were out of work. Thereafter the increase in employment, while never spectacular, was steady (provided seasonal variations, stemming from the fact that fewer people are generally employed in the building and other trades in the winter months, are ignored). Only in 1937–8 was the trend disturbed, as the trade cycle turned downwards, but this was short-lived. Nevertheless in 1939 there were still a million and a half people out of work.

Average unemployment totals	
1932 – 2,700,000	1936 – 1,600,000
1933 – 2,500,000	1937 – 1,500,000
1934 – 2,200,000	1938 – 1,900,000
1935 – 2,000,000	1939 – 1,500,000

These figures are useful: although they tell us about only one aspect of the economy in the 1930s, they show that there was undoubtedly some sort of recovery. But, as *national* totals, they tell us nothing about the regional pattern of employment.

b) The Depressed Areas

The staple industries, already suffering from structural unemployment in the 1920s, were badly hit by the depression of the early 1930s. Export orders fell, and consequently these industries suffered unemployment levels far higher than the national averages. In 1932, when a national average of 22 per cent of workers were unemployed, 35 per cent of coalminers were out of work, 46 per cent of iron and steel workers and 62 per cent of shipbuilders and repairers. In individual towns, especially those economically dependent on a single ailing industry, totals were especially high. In 1934 62 per cent of workers were unemployed in Merthyr Tydfil in South Wales which was dependent on mining. In Jarrow, in the North East, where Palmers' shipbuilding yard had closed down, 73 per cent were out of a job in 1935. ('There is no escape anywhere in Jarrow from its prevailing misery', noted J.B. Priestley. Ellen Wilkinson entitled her 'life-story' of the place *The Town That Was Murdered*.)

For the rest of the 1930s the staple industries continued to suffer from economic depression. Indeed, in some ways the situation became worse than ever. In the cotton industry, for example, where production had already fallen by 25 per cent in 1910–20, and then by almost 50 per cent in the following decade, exports fell from 3,800 million square yards in 1929 to 2,000 million in 1937. India, which had been the great market for Lancashire textiles in the previous century, was now exporting cotton goods to Britain. It was a similar story with shipbuilding. Orders for British ships dropped badly in the 1930s, so that in 1936 Britain actually imported more ships than it exported.

The concentration of the staple industries in certain areas of the country meant that unemployment in the 1930s was a regional phenomenon, once the worst of the depression was over. There were exceptions (pockets of prosperity) within this broad pattern, but these (like Halifax in Yorkshire, centre of a flourishing machine tool trade) were the proverbial exceptions that prove the rule. The 'depressed areas' were born (see the map on page 66).

The 'optimists' point out that even in these areas of the country there were some signs of growth. Steel production, for example, rose from a trough of 5.2 million tons in 1932 to reach 7 million in 1933 and 13 million in 1937. Britain's share of world output was rising and the industry was being made more efficient. There were also important advances in the coal industry. British pits could not regain their prewar export markets, and nor did they produce as much in the 1930s as at the end of the 1920s, but productivity reached new heights. Output per man rose by over one-third between 1924 and 1938, and by the end of the decade over 60 per cent of coal was cut by machinery. However, such developments need to be seen in a

Unemployment in Britain in 1937

European context. Productivity increased at least twice as rapidly over the same years in continental mines as in Britain. In the Ruhr, in Germany, 97 per cent of coal was cut by mechanical means as early as 1934.

c) Economic Revival: the New and Service Industries

There is disagreement about just how badly the Great Depression hit Britain. The 'optimists' point out that whereas world output fell by almost 30 per cent between 1929 and 1932, Britain's declined by only half this figure, while the 'pessimists' reply that this was simply due to the fact that the British economy had not undergone a boom in the late-1920s: having risen less steeply than its rivals, it had less far to fall. All are agreed, however, that there was a significant revival of output in the 1930s, as the following table indicates.

Index of Production

1929 – 100 (an index figure)	1934 – 104
1930 – 92	1935 – 110
1931 – 84	1936 – 118
1932 – 85	1937 – 124
1933 – 93	

We can thus see that between 1932 and 1937 industrial production rose by 46 per cent. One feature of this was the continued development of the electricity industry. In 1930 one in three houses was supplied with electricity, but in 1939 two out of three houses were wired for supply. By this time 325,000 people worked for the electricity industry, and probably the same number were employed in electrical engineering, helping to produce the new range of electrically-powered consumer goods. The consumption of electricity doubled between 1931 and 1937. The number of electric cookers sold increased from 75,000 in 1930 to 250,000 in 1935, and the number of radios from 500,000 in 1930 to 2 million in 1937.

The motor-vehicle industry was another success story of the 1930s. Three firms – Morris at Cowley in Oxford, Ford at Dagenham in Essex and Austin at Longbridge in Birmingham – dominated production, and output rose from 95,000 vehicles in 1923 to over half a million in 1937. By 1939, 400,000 people were employed in the motor industry, and during the Thirties the number of vehicles on the road doubled, from 1.5 to 3 million. The millionth Morris Minor was produced at Cowley just before the Second World War. (Deaths on the roads peaked at 7,300 in 1934, the year the driving test was instituted.)

The aircraft industry also expanded considerably, at Coventry and Bristol, and so did chemical giants like Imperial Chemical Industries (ICI), which even set up a factory at Jarrow in the late 1930s. More typically, however, the new industries tended to be sited in the South East and the Midlands (see the map on page 66), rather than in the depressed areas of the country: 80 per cent of new factories built between 1932 and 1937 were in Greater London, by which time about one-fifth of Britain's population lived within a 15-mile radius of Charing Cross (with consequent problems of congestion). Not only did the new factories provide jobs in this area, but so too did the new service industries that grew up as a consequence – retailing, insurance, advertising, and forms of entertainment such as the cinema. Such service industries increased their workforce even during the worst years of the depression.

d) The Housing Boom

Another source of growth in the economy was the 'housing boom'. In the 1920s an average of 150,000 new houses had been completed each year in England and Wales, but from 1930 onwards there was a substantial increase. Even during the worst years of depression (1931–2), 200,000 houses were constructed each year in England and Wales, and for the rest of the decade significantly more dwellings were erected. In the Thirties as a whole, 2.7 million were built.

There were several reasons for this growth: building costs (and especially the price of imported timber) fell during the depression and also the construction industry became more efficient. In addition, investment in building societies rose eightfold in the interwar period, so that it became relatively easy to obtain cheap mortgages (at around 4.5 per cent interest) and now they could be extended over a longer period (typically 25 years rather than 16). The 1930s have been called 'probably the most favourable period for house purchase in the twentieth century'. Priced at around £450 for a semi-detached house, twice the annual salary of a professional man, new houses were now within the range of most middle-class and some working-class families.

Not surprisingly, the number of workers employed in the building industry increased by almost one-third in the 1930s, while the housing boom also led to further employment in trades supplying building materials. New houses were wired for electricity, and so the electricity industry was also stimulated. Often the new houses were sited in the suburbs of major cities, and as a result the transportation system (the 'economic infrastructure') – including new electric railways in the South – was modernised.

e) 1937–8: a Temporary Brake

In the autumn of 1937 the business cycle dipped, and the economy seemed about to go into recession. In the worst months of 1938 unemployment reached almost 2 million, and in the year as a whole industrial production fell and the balance of payments deficit worsened. But the downswing proved short-lived, mainly because the government had embarked on a rearmament programme that stimulated industry. Between 1935 and 1939 rearmament created around a million new jobs. Hence the interwar period ended with a relatively buoyant economy. Even the number of unemployed had declined. In 1939 an average of 7.9 per cent of the insured workforce were unemployed, the lowest figure since 1920. Yet even so, a million or more people were out of a job until the spring of 1940. The main economic problem of the whole interwar period had not been solved.

6 Causes of Economic Recovery

> **KEY ISSUE** What combination of factors best explains Britain's recovery from cyclical unemployment?

a) The Trade Cycle

Most historians agree that there was a recovery after the Great Depression, but there is no consensus about the causes of this upturn. Some say that the 'natural' recovery of the trade cycle was responsible. This view is supported by the fact that the autumn of 1937 saw the ending of the upward curve of the cycle – a sure sign that recovery was at least partly cyclical – and also by the fact that the recovery was on a worldwide scale. According to this view, there is no great mystery about such recovery as occurred: it owed much more to external factors than to any internal strength of the British economy. It has even been said, by the pessimists, that, without the artificial stimulus provided by rearmament, unemployment might have risen to 3 million by 1939. However, most historians would argue that there were other causes of the recovery besides the operation of the trade cycle.

b) The New Industries

Several historians have pointed to the dynamic role of the new industries in producing recovery. But there are problems with this view. First there is the question of definition. What exactly was a 'new' industry? Some industries which have been classified as new (such as rayon production) were very much out-growths of 'old' industries (textiles, in the case of rayon). There has also been a tendency to define 'new' as 'expanding' – in which case it is scarcely surprising that the 'new' industries seem to have spearheaded industrial growth. Above all, it has been said that they constituted too small a portion of British industry to account for the recovery: they were responsible for only 7 per cent of employment in 1934 and for only about 20 per cent of output in 1935. They were also sometimes far less efficient than is generally supposed: the chemical giant ICI, for instance, invested £20 million in a fertiliser plant – an amount equivalent to one-third of all capital investment in manufacturing industry in that year – but soon had to write off the whole amount as a total failure. Furthermore, the newer industries may have grown most strongly after the vital 1932–4 period in which the depression ended. They may thus have sustained rather than started the recovery.

Nevertheless, it is clear that the new industries were a growing and significant force within the economy, even though the staple industries constituted a larger part of the total economy. (While the staple industries accounted for 37 per cent of British industrial production in 1924 and 28 per cent in 1935, the corresponding figures for new industries are 14 and 20 per cent.) Did the new industries lift the economy out of recession? Most historians would judge that while they probably did not, they nevertheless contributed to recovery. The roles of the electricity and car industries were especially important.

c) The Housing Boom

The 'housing boom' has also been seen as a major factor in British recovery. It undoubtedly had a significant effect, and by 1935 (the peak year for construction) a high proportion of all investment in Britain went into housing. Building and allied trades absorbed an extra 750,000 workers between 1932 and 1934. But perhaps this factor was in turn made possible by others, including population movements, mortgage availability and low interest rates (see page 132). House-building also involved so many allied industries (cement, electricity, plumbing, and so on) that it has been said that building alone cannot have been responsible for recovery: the allied trades must have already been in relatively good shape. Nevertheless few would deny that the housing boom was another important factor in Britain's economic growth in the 1930s.

d) Affluence and Consumer Spending

Clearly Britain's economic recovery from the Great Depression depended in large measure on the ability and willingness of people to spend – to purchase new houses and buy the increasing range of consumer goods that were on offer. To a large degree, the 1930s saw a 'consumer-led' recovery. This in turn depended on the existence of a greater degree of 'disposable income' (that is, a surplus after expenditure on basic necessities) among British people (see page 71).

A major factor in this higher standard of living was a fall in the cost of goods that resulted from more efficient methods of production and also from a steep fall in the price of imported raw materials. The 'terms of trade' (a comparison between the relative costs of Britain's exports and imports) moved in Britain's favour in the 1930s: for a given volume of exports Britain could purchase an expanding volume of imports. For example, in 1936 Britain was importing almost exactly the same volume of goods as in 1929 but their cost was 32 per cent less. Put another way, Britain's new higher standard of living was purchased at the price of lower standards in 'third world' countries.

7 British Society

> **KEY ISSUES** How did the different classes fare in Britain between the wars?

a) The wealthy

'England,' wrote George Orwell in 1940, 'is the most class-ridden country under the sun. It is a land of snobbery and privilege'. Certainly many among the upper classes continued to live a life of conspicuous consumption, and even in December 1939, when Britain was again at war with Germany, the consumption of luxury goods, like French perfume and champagne, was high. Bookings for Christmas banquets were not much lower than usual. There were more British millionaires than ever before in the 1930s. By the end of the decade Britain's wealthiest 1 per cent owned 55 per cent of the wealth. In fact, their share had declined, as before the First World War they had owned 69 per cent of the wealth – but the beneficiaries were also the wealthy, so that in 1937 the top 5 per cent owned no less than 79 per cent of the country's wealth. As we can see from studying wills, three-quarters of Britons left possessions and property worth less than £100 when they died, and many left nothing at all.

The numbers attending private, fee-paying schools increased by a third between the wars, a sure sign of middle-class affluence. (Parents generally thought it was money well spent, and it has been calculated that nearly half of the 'top jobs' in Britain were filled by the products of the five most prestigious 'public schools'.) Taxation was relatively low, and in 1931 one in every five households, almost all middle-class, employed one or more full-time, live-in domestic servants. Lower middle-class families would have one maid (often dubbed 'slavey'); and those that could not afford such a necessity would have a 'daily'. Middle-class period people experienced significant improvements in their housing, consumption of food and health – in short, in their living standards. Yet such benefits were not spread evenly throughout society.

b) The Working Classes

The proportion of manual workers in Britain's population declined in the twentieth century (from 75 per cent in 1911 to 70 in 1931 and 65 in 1951), but the working classes remained the largest single group. The majority of them became wealthier in the interwar years. The Ministry of Labour established that in 1938 an 'average family' had double the real income of a family in 1913–14. Those in work in the 1930s were progressively better off as the decade proceeded since, although wage rates fell, continuing deflation meant that the cost of living fell more steeply. The result was a significant rise in living standards. During the Thirties, average real wages probably rose by about 15 per cent.

Another factor was the smaller size of British families. Women marrying in the 1880s had had an average of 4.6 children each; but in the 1920s, owing to a greater use of contraception, that figure had fallen to 2.2. The working classes still had the largest families, but by the 1930s 80 per cent of all families had three or fewer children. Smaller family size meant greater disposable income, as can be seen in the increased amounts and variety of food that was being consumed. More money was spent on food, and yet the proportion of the family budget spent on nutrition fell. Partly as a result of this, partly because of better medical inspection and treatment, life expectancy increased:

Expectation of Life in England and Wales		
Men	**Women**	**Year**
52 years	55 years	1912
61 years	66 years	1938

There was also a significant decline in infant mortality:

Infant mortality (under 12 months) per 1,000 live births	
1900	142
1920	82
1940	61

On average children became taller and heavier, and puberty began earlier.

The greater affluence of Britons, and their greater leisure time, can also be seen in the greater numbers of consumer goods that could be afforded and in the amounts spent on entertainment and holidays. Expenditure on tobacco grew from £42 million in 1914 to £204 in 1939, and in 1938 10 million Britons staked £40 million on the football pools. According to the *Economist*, gambling was Britain's second biggest industry. In 1936/7 31.5 million Britons attended Football League matches in England. The 1930s were also the heyday of the cinema: by the end of the decade over 20 million tickets were sold each week at Britain's 5,000 cinemas. In addition, three-quarters of all families by the mid-1930s had access to a radio. Scarcely less important to many people was the annual holiday. During the 1930s the number of people entitled to a paid holiday increased from about 1.5 million to over 11 million, and by the end of the decade around 20 million people visited the seaside every year. Billy Butlin opened his first holiday camps in the years before the Second World War. The number of jobs in entertainment and sport grew, between 1930 and 1937, from 65,000 to 116,000, while those in hotels and restaurants increased from 300,000 to 380,000.

c) Poverty

There were significant improvements in the average standard of living in Britain in the 1930s. Yet averages can disguise wide variations, and undoubtedly poverty existed – and when benefits were cut by 10 per cent in 1931 (see page 130) it increased. Surveys established that there were wide variations in the health of Britons in different socio-economic groups. For instance, public schoolboys were on average 4 inches (c. 10 cm) taller than those from poorer families. People in more affluent areas were also likely to live longer. In some industrial cities the death rate was 50 per cent higher than the average for England and Wales.

In addition, infant mortality was much higher in some parts of the country than others.

Infant mortality rates (per 1,000 live births) in 1935	
Home Counties	42
Glamorgan	63
Jarrow	114

Charities reported a definite decline in children's health during the worst of the depression, in 1931 and 1932. Rates for maternal mortality (i.e. for women dying during childbirth) did not fall in the interwar period, and reached their worst point in 1934, and this was to a large extent because of disproportionately high rates among the poor. Rates in Durham were over six times as high as in Middlesex. A report by the Pilgrim Trust, published in 1938, estimated that about 3,000 women a year were dying in childbirth in the depressed areas because of poor nutrition and stress. In addition, many women were 'literally starving themselves in order to feed and clothe the children reasonably well'.

In 1936 an expert nutritionist, John Boyd Orr, analysed the food consumption of different socio-economic groups:

ı The consumption of bread and potatoes is practically uniform throughout the different income level groups. Consumption of milk, eggs, fruit,
vegetables, meat and fish rises with income. Thus, in the poorest group
the average consumption of milk, including tinned milk, is equivalent to
5 1.8 pints per head per week; in the wealthiest group 5.5 pints. The
poorest group consume 1.5 eggs per week; the wealthiest 4.5. The
poorest spend 2.4d on fruit; the wealthiest 1s 8d.
    An examination of the composition of the diets of the different
groups shows that the degree of adequacy of health increases as
ıo incomes rise. The average diet of the poorest group, comprising 4.4
million people, is, by the standard adopted, deficient in every con-
stituent examined. The second group, comprising 9 million people, is
adequate in protein, fat and carbohydrate, but deficient in all the

vitamins and minerals considered ... A review of the state of health of
15 the people of the different groups suggests that, as income increases,
disease and death-rate decrease, children grow more quickly, adult
stature is greater and general health and physique improve.

A journalist, Dudley Barker, could see the effects of low standards in
South Wales in 1936:

1 I saw a man, prematurely old, crouching over a stove in a dark room,
the light from the fire touching his sunken features as he coughed and
coughed. I saw women, bending over wash-tubs, shaking with unstrung
nerves from the conditions in which they were forced to live. One
5 woman sank into a chair, her form wasted, and death written more
plainly on her face than I have ever seen it. Her unemployed husband
stood by, trying with a tattered shawl to warm a baby three months old.
He smiled proudly down at it. His teeth were rotten with decay. A few
blocks away I found a widow and four sons in a house that was literally
10 crumbling ... Rats breed there, and the woman told me how she had to
chase them from her rooms.

One of the most precise investigations undertaken into poverty was
conducted by Seebohm Rowntree, who had shown in 1899 that 28 per
cent of the population of York had been poverty-stricken (see page
14). Now, in 1936, he demonstrated that – despite the extension of
unemployment insurance in the interwar years to cover virtually the
whole population, with added sums for dependants – levels of benefit
were inadequate to keep men and their families above the poverty
line. Almost three-quarters of unemployed men and their families
lived in poverty. He now defined the 'poverty line' more generously
than he had done previously: to the cost of bare subsistence needs he
added 3s (15p) for luxuries such as beer, tobacco and a newspaper.
But even so he insisted that he was being far from extravagant.
Whereas earlier he had found 28 per cent of York's population in poverty, he now – on the criterion of his new poverty line – found that 18
per cent (or 31.1 per cent of the working-class population) were poor,
half in 'primary poverty' (because of the inadequacy of their wages),
half in secondary (because of unwise expenditure).

According to Rowntree, there had been improvements, but there
was no cause for complacency:

1 The economic condition of the workers is better by 30 per cent than
in 1899, though working hours are shorter. Housing is immeasurably
better, health is better, education is better ... It is gratifying that so
much progress has been achieved, but if instead of looking backward we
5 look forward, then we see how far the standard of living of many
workers falls short of any standard which could be regarded, even for
the time being, as satisfactory. Great though the progress made during
the last forty years has been, there is no cause for satisfaction in the fact
that in a country so rich as England, over 30 per cent of the workers in

10 a typical provincial city should have incomes so small that it is beyond their means to live even at the stringently economical level adopted as a minimum in this survey, nor in the fact that almost half the children of working-class parents spend the first five years of their lives in poverty and that almost a third of them live below the poverty line for ten years
15 or more.

Surveys of other towns and cities told a similar story. George Orwell visited the north of England in February and March 1936, and he was appalled by the sheer ugliness of the industrial landscape, and by the squalor, poor diets, inadequate housing and human waste and misery that confronted him. Yet he found the reaction of the unemployed and the low paid to their predicament to be admirable:

1 A working man does not disintegrate under the strain of poverty ... Life is still fairly normal, more normal that one really has the right to expect. Families are impoverished but the family-system has not broken up. The people are in effect living a reduced version of their former lives.
5 Instead of raging against their destiny they have made things tolerable by lowering their standards.

But they don't necessarily lower their standards by cutting out luxuries and concentrating on necessities; more often it is the other way about ... It is quite likely that fish and chips, art-silk stockings, tinned
10 salmon, cut-price chocolate ..., the movies, the radio, strong tea and the Football Pools have between them averted a revolution.

d) Women

We have seen that women bore the full brunt of poverty in the 1930s. We might also expect that, with the interwar slump, women would be likely to lose their jobs. This was very much the case. The Restoration of Pre-war Practices Act of 1919 meant that most women lost their places in industry to returning soldiers, and married women were among the first to be dismissed during the slumps and recessions of the interwar period. To make matters worse, the government in 1931 deprived married women of entitlement to unemployment benefit.

Long-term trends show that the First World War had not produced significant changes in working patterns (though it should be noted that in total more women were employed).

Women in Paid Employment

Year	Single	Married	All Women	Female Earnings
1911	70%	10%	35% (5.2 m)	44% of male
1931	71%	10%	34% (6.3m)	48% of male

It was still quite normal for women nurses and clerical workers to be forced to resign when they married. Nor had the type of work undertaken by women changed much. More women were employed in domestic service than in any other sphere, and only 0.5 per cent of women continued their education beyond the age of 18. Some women had received the vote in 1918, and ten years later women became eligible for the vote on the same terms as men. This was bound to happen sooner or later: the fact that women could vote at 30, whereas men were eligible at 21, was clearly an anomaly. Yet parliament was probably the more willing to enfranchise women aged 21–29 because the original extension of the franchise had produced so few results. In the seven elections of the interwar period, women MPs only reached double figures twice. The number peaked in 1931 when they won 15 seats, out of a total of 615. Issues of especial concern to women, like birth control and equal pay, did not figure prominently on the political agenda. There were some changes – for instance, it became easier for women to obtain divorces – but radical feminists were dismayed that no women's political party appeared.

There was a 'cult of domesticity' in 1918–39. Governments encouraged women to stay at home and breed healthy babies. This was also the message of dozens of new magazines for women. *Good Housekeeping* was the best-seller, its title conveying its message with precision. The goal of the 'natural' woman was married bliss and motherhood in an ideal home. Those who had babies out of wedlock were often sent to special institutions and their babies put up for adoption.

Many feminist historians deplore the interwar years as a period of missed opportunities and continued male domination. Yet several provisos should be made. First, there was a greater admission of women into the professions. The number of women doctors, for instance, grew from 500 in 1914 to 2,500 in 1935. Second, the trend towards smaller families benefited women. Third, it is perfectly understandable if many women preferred housework to factory work, given the arduous nature of the latter. Finally, it should be noted that a higher proportion of women worked in Britain at this time than in any other European country.

8 The 1930s: a Conclusion

> **KEY ISSUE** What verdict should we reach on Britain's economic performance in this decade?

Mass unemployment was a personal tragedy for millions of people in the 1930s. Lives were blighted and human potential was wasted. Many of the unemployed felt that, to the politicians at Westminster, they were merely statistics. Unfortunately it is easy for historians to consider them in the same way, as so many units in an economic equation. There is a perennial danger that historians – and especially economic historians, to whom individual life-stories can seldom be as significant as large-scale (macro-)economic trends – will fail to see the human reality that underlies their studies. It often requires a conscious effort to realise the human significance of statistical and other data.

Unemployment should also be at the centre of our study of British economic performance for another reason: it reveals that the economy was operating at considerably below optimum level. As we have seen, there are various ways of assessing British economic performance – in comparison with that of its competitors, for instance, or with other periods in British history. Another way is to construct a 'counterfactual model' (as opposed to the 'factual' record of what was achieved). This is a highly complicated undertaking. It involves assessing how Britain could have performed economically, given its raw materials, its population, the availability of markets, consumption habits and so on. The clearest fact of all to emerge from the construction of such a model is that an economy cannot operate at anything like full efficiency when over 10 per cent of its workers are unemployed. Well over a million workers were unproductive in the 1930s and had to be supported by unemployment benefit. In addition, they were unable to stimulate economic growth because they could not afford to buy many goods or services. The unemployed were thus an economic liability, whereas in work they would have been an asset. It can also be argued that the existence of such a large number of unemployed people tended to keep down wage rates for those in work, since workers who refused to accept existing wage levels could be replaced by the 'reserve army of the unemployed'. As a result, living standards in general were lower than they otherwise might have been.

There were other economic failures as well. The staple industries declined significantly, and in addition the balance of payments situation was unfavourable. From 1930 to 1938 there was an annual average deficit on visible trade of £255 million, which was only partially offset by annual surpluses from invisible earnings averaging £216 million.

Yet no one should deny that there were also many economic successes in the 1930s, especially in the growth of new consumer goods industries. Those who praise the economic performance of the 1930s would say that the economy was undergoing a painful but necessary period of economic readjustment: in other words, the economy had to switch from producing what people did not want to supplying what they did. Thus unemployment, while a personal tragedy to those thrown out of work, can be seen as an inevitable consequence of a necessary economic reorientation. According to this view, the 'decline' of the staple industries should be seen not as a failure of the 1930s but, paradoxically, almost as a success. The staple industries had to decline, to employ fewer people and to match their output to consumers' needs. The key issue was whether as they became leaner they also became fitter and more competitive. The iron and steel industry undoubtedly did.

The annual growth rate for British industry in the 1930s was between 2.3 and 3.3 per cent (a substantial achievement) and between 1932 and 1937 industrial output rose by almost 50 per cent. Britain may have fallen behind its rivals in industrial growth in the 1920s, but this was not the case in the 1930s. Its rate of growth outstripped that of the United States and France. By 1939 Britain was fourth in the world table of industrial producers, behind the USA, the USSR and Germany, all larger and 'naturally' stronger competitors. Behind Britain – a long way behind – came rivals of more equal size and resources. In 1939 Britain was producing twice as much as France, two and a half times as much as Japan, and over three times as much as Italy. Britain's share of world trade in the 1930s varied from year to year (9.36 per cent was the lowest in 1931, 11.08 per cent the highest in 1935), but it had very probably ceased to decline.

9 The Interwar Period as a Whole

> **KEY ISSUE** What overall conclusions should we reach about the 1918–39 period?

a) Agriculture

Agriculture was a small sector of the economy, producing no more than 4 per cent of Britain's national income and employing between 5 and 7 per cent of the British workforce, but it should not be entirely overlooked. Before 1914 British agriculture had been in decline: prices were low and around 55 per cent (by value) of all foods consumed in Britain were imported. During the war, when imports were cut back, production of food had expanded rapidly and it was hoped that in the postwar period food production could be permanently increased so that the import bill might be reduced. In fact these hopes were not fulfilled. World food prices fell in 1921 and again in 1929, acting as a disincentive to farmers. Food production in Britain increased by about 4 per cent between 1925 and 1930, largely owing to higher yields per acre, but by the latter date the percentage of food that was imported had risen to 60.

In the 1930s there was again increased output. Between 1931 and 1937 production rose by about one-sixth. This was largely because attempts were made to utilise more scientific methods (thus improving yields) and to introduce greater mechanisation. The number of tractors in England and Wales increased from 16,500 in 1925 to

40,000 in 1937, while over the same period the number of working horses declined; but even so there were still about 20 times more horses than tractors in the mid-1930s. Indeed, Britain had one of the least mechanised farming systems of the economically advanced nations. It was not until the Second World War that there was a real modernisation of British agriculture. Between 1939 and 1945 the number of tractors and combine harvesters on British farms increased by 400 per cent.

In the 1930s under the stimulus of government subsidies of over £100 million a year, there were modest increases in farming efficiency. The number of farm workers fell by about a third (from 7 to 5 per cent of the total workforce), the acreage under cultivation fell marginally (by about 5 per cent), and yet production increased. At the end of the period Britain imported about 50 per cent of its food, less than before the First World War. There had therefore been increases in productivity. Yet, although British agriculture between the wars was certainly not a story of failure, few have ventured to call it a success.

b) Economy and Society

Britain's industrial performance between 1918 and 1939 was very varied, and it is thus very difficult to generalise about it. Indeed, even to talk about what happened in 'staple' and 'new' industries is to ignore the very real differences that existed between different trades within these two broad sectors – and within each trade there were firms that performed very differently. There were also considerable regional variations, while the fluctuations of the trade cycle meant that there was considerable change over time, rather than a linear pattern towards greater poverty or affluence. The diversity was such that evidence can be provided for any number of generalisations about British industrial performance. We must therefore be cautious and qualified in our assessment.

The interwar period was a paradoxical one economically. Many people began to experience affluence for the first time, while others were condemned to life on the dole. In 1933 the novelist J.B. Priestley toured England:

1 I had seen England. I had seen a lot of Englands. How many? At once
   three disengaged themselves from the shifting mass. There was, first,
   Old England, the country of the cathedrals and manor houses and inns,
   of Parson and Squire ... We all know this England, which at its best
5 cannot be improved upon in this world. That is, as a country to lounge
   about in ... It has long ceased to earn its own living ...
      Then, I decided, there is the nineteenth-century England, the indus-
   trial England of coal, iron, steel, cotton, wool, railways; of thousands of
   rows of little houses all alike ... This England ... is not being added to

10 and has no new life poured into it ... It provided a good parade ground
for tough, enterprising men, who would build their factories in the
knowledge that the world was waiting for their products, and who also
knew that once they had accumulated a tidy fortune they could slip out
of this mucky England of their making ...

15 The third England, I concluded, was the new post-war England,
belonging far more to the age itself than to the particular island.
America, I supposed, was its real birth-place. This is the England of arte-
rial and by-pass roads, of filling stations and factories that look like exhi-
bition buildings, of giant cinemas and dance halls and cafes, bungalows

20 and tiny garages, cocktail bars, Woolworths, motor-coaches, wireless,
hiking, factory girls looking like actresses, greyhound racing and dirt
tracks, swimming pools and everything given away for cigarette
coupons ... It is a large-scale, mass-production job, with cut prices. You
could almost accept Woolworths as its symbol.

Priestley spotted three Englands. Perhaps there was others too,
including that of the very rich and that of the poverty-stricken. In
addition, he said nothing of Wales, Scotland or Northern Ireland. It
is undoubtedly preferable to stress the variety of Britain between the
wars rather than to convey a one-sided picture of affluence or
depression. There were riches and poverty, boom and bust. It was
both 'the best of times' and 'the worst of times'. These phrases can of
course be applied to virtually every period in human history: at all
times there are positive and negative features to human society. Every
buoyant economy contains elements of stagnation, and every declining economy nevertheless exhibits some progressive traits. The key
question is always the relative importance of the positive and negative
features. In the interwar years both were vital. There were probably
twice as many coalminers as car-workers in the mid-1930s, and thus we
cannot ignore the relatively stagnant sectors of the economy. The new
industries, on the other hand, while more capital-intensive, contributed significantly to Britain's production. For millions of people
the interwar years were a time of poverty and distress, and yet for millions of other people there was unparalleled affluence and opportunity. We must therefore give virtually equal weight to poverty and
riches and reach a conclusion which is not indefinite or vague but
decidedly two-sided.

The other issue to be addressed is the overall degree of change in
the economy by the end of the interwar period. It is true that the
trade cycle ruled out any straight-line economic progress; but on
the other hand one cycle was followed by another, and by the end of
the interwar period it was clear that the economy had undergone significant development. For this reason, there was also important social
progress. Britons on average were better housed, better fed, better
educated, were healthier and lived longer. The depressed areas were
undoubtedly a national scandal, and poverty existed on a mass scale.

But, in absolute terms, the poor were less poor than they had been. The unemployed in 1939 had very similar living standards to those of employed unskilled workers in 1914. Greater affluence also made possible improved social services. A new pension scheme (compulsory and without a means test) was introduced in 1925, unemployment insurance was extended, and local authorities – employing 2,300 doctors and 5,300 nurses by 1935 – undertook the inspection and medical treatment of children aged 5–14. Significant legislation included the 1936 Midwives Act, which obliged local authorities to provide trained midwives. Total spending on social services by the national and local authorities grew from £67.5 million a year just before the First World War to £475 million a year just before the Second World War.

Overall economic change also meant that Britain was no longer pre-eminently an exporting economy. Most of the growth generated in the interwar period had been due to domestic consumption. This was an important change. Exports from the 'staple industries' (a term that had become an anachronism) had fallen alarmingly, and indeed not since 1851 had Lancashire exported so little. Exports never recovered to their 1913 level between the wars, and the 1929 level was not equalled for the rest of the period, despite the fact that by 1937 British economic production was 20 per cent higher than in 1929 (see the table on page 67).

The Victorian economy had indeed 'crashed in ruins' between the wars. But another economy had taken its place, based on new mass production techniques and capable of producing higher rates of growth than in 1900–13. Despite large-scale unemployment, total output per head of the population probably grew between 1924 and 1937 by a third, faster in fact than in the heyday of Victorian England. This was a substantial achievement, especially since more people were now engaged in the non-productive 'service' industries, an achievement obscured for too long by the tenacious, one-sided popular image of the 1930s as 'the devil's decade' of unemployment and political failure.

For a time in the 1930s Britain's relative economic decline seemed to have been halted. Britain had come to rest, after a decline (*vis-à-vis* its rivals) that had been under way since the 1880s. Or so it seemed. In retrospect, we know it was merely a pause before another catastrophic world war and further decline. But the pause was a measure of the economic success of the interwar years. Perhaps much more might have been achieved. It is often said that even the most progressive British firms tended to neglect management training and failed to invest sufficiently in industrial research. In addition, we can only wonder at how much greater the success might have been, in economic and social terms, had governments tackled Britain's economic problems more effectively and had industrial relations been more harmonious.

Summary Diagram
The Inter-war Years: An Economy in Decline?

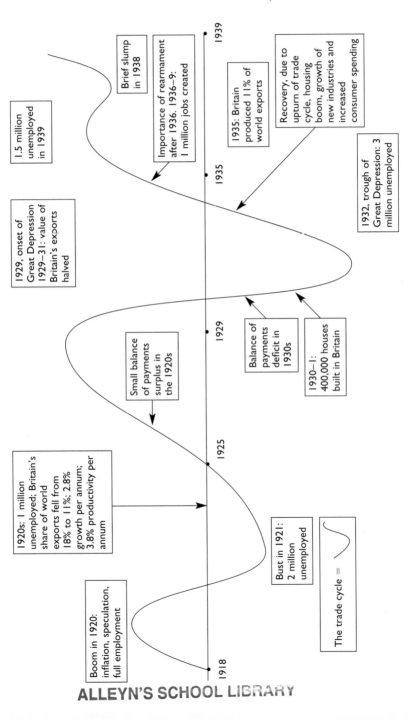

1939

Brief slump
in 1938

Importance of rearmament
after 1936. 1936–9:
1 million jobs created

1.5 million
unemployed
in 1939

1935: Britain
produced 11% of
world exports

Recovery, due to
upturn of trade
cycle, housing
boom, growth of
new industries and
increased
consumer spending

1935

1929, onset of
Great Depression
1929–31: value of
Britain's exports
halved

1932, trough of
Great Depression: 3
million unemployed

Small balance
of payments
surplus in
the 1920s

1929

Balance of
payments
deficit in
1930s

1930–1:
400,000 houses
built in Britain

1925

1920s: 1 million
unemployed; Britain's
share of world
exports fell from
18% to 11%; 2.8%
growth per annum;
3.8% productivity per
annum

Bust in 1921:
2 million
unemployed

The trade cycle =

Boom in 1920:
inflation, speculation,
full employment

1918

Working on Chapter 4

You need a detailed set of notes on this chapter. The headings and sub-headings should help you to organise your notes efficiently. As in previous chapters, the concluding sections are worth particular attention. Here you should think through the issues as thoroughly as possible and formulate your own views. Do not tamely accept the views of the author. (Is he 'sitting on the fence'?)

Finally, a word of warning. It is very easy when making notes on economic developments to lose the significance of figures by being too brief. If you are dealing with output, for instance, always remember to note not merely production totals but the period over which they are measured. Such accuracy is essential: it makes the difference between conveying sense and nonsense. You might write down that in a certain industry production increased by 10 per cent – but does this mean per annum or over a set period of years? Also, remember to specify which units things are measured in: there is a big difference between pounds, kilograms, tons, and so on.

Answering structured and essay questions on Chapter 4

First, consider the following structured question:

a) Define the terms 'cyclical unemployment' and 'structural unemployment'. (*5 marks*)
b) What were the causes of each in Britain between the wars? (*15 marks*)
c) What factors led to Britain's economic recovery from depression in the 1930s. (*20 marks*)

This chapter also provides material for essay (A2) questions. A wide variety of questions can be asked on the interwar period as a whole. For instance:

1. To what extent should the period 1918–39 be seen as one of British economic decline?
2. Were the interwar years characterised by depression or reconstruction for the British economy?
3. Account for the persistently high levels of unemployment that existed in Britain from 1921 to 1939.

Construct an essay plan for each of these titles. In particular, work out ways of dividing up the material into manageable sections, on each of which you could write a paragraph. It is also worth spending time thinking about the main interpretation you would put forward to answer questions 1 and 2. Both of these questions ask about the relative importance of the 'positive' and 'negative' aspects of the economy. Would you give them equal weight or assign more prominence to one or the other? Remember the importance of establishing the criteria on which judgements are based. The third title is different. It demands a knowledge of the economic factors that produced both structural and cyclical unemployment, but it would also be wise to bring in material on the government policies that affected employment levels (an issue dealt with in Chapter 6).

Questions can also centre on the 1920s; but far more common are questions on the 1930s:

4. 'By 1939 Britain had only partially recovered from the depression of the early 1930s.' Discuss.
5. Do you agree that Britain's recovery from the depression of the 1930s was regional rather than national?
6. Why did poverty exist on such a large scale in Britain in the 1930s?

Variants of these questions are extremely common. It is worth thinking how you might tackle the final paragraph of each of them. Try to provide succinct six to eight line conclusions. Remember that your answer must reflect the different types of questions asked. With the first type, which merely asks you to discuss a quotation, you are given a wide degree of latitude: but, even so, you must centre your discussion on the statement quoted. Do you agree with the view? If so, say so directly, and then comment on the degree of partial recovery as well as its sources. Perhaps you might think that 'partial' recovery for Britain as a whole stemmed from 'complete' recovery in certain areas, or maybe you think the word 'recovery' is misleading in its implication of a 'return to a former condition'. For the second question, you obviously have to answer a direct question: you can say yes or no; or, more likely, you will say 'yes' (to some extent and in certain respects) and 'no' (in others). For the third question, you must find a form of words to define the extent of poverty and match the causal factors with this.

It is not easy to formulate adequate conclusions – all that is stressed here is the absolute necessity of tackling the key issues, instead of spoiling an essay by failing to address them.

Source-based questions on Chapter 4

1. Poverty in the 1930s

Read the extracts from John Boyd Orr, Dudley Barker, Seebohm Rowntree and George Orwell on pages 73, 74, 74–5 and 75 respectively. Answer the following questions:

a) What possible explanations are there for the inadequate diets of the lowest-paid workers, exposed by Boyd Orr? (5 marks)
b) How convincing do you find Barker's depiction of poverty? What further information, ideally, would you like him to provide you with? (5 marks)

c) What did Rowntree mean by 'the stringently economical level adopted as a minimum in this survey' (page 75, lines 11–12)? (*3 marks*)

d) Why did Rowntree draw particular attention to children living in poverty? (*3 marks*)

e) Explain why, according to Orwell, the poor did not cut out luxuries and focus on necessities. (*5 marks*)

f) Use your knowledge to estimate how complete a picture of the life of the poor in 1930s' Britain these extracts provide. (*9 marks*)

5 The General Strike and Industrial Relations between the Wars

POINTS TO CONSIDER

The General Strike of 1926 is easily the most important industrial dispute of the period, and you need to understand why it occurred and why it lasted so short a time. But we can only see this strike in perspective if we study it as part of a longer period. Hence do not neglect the years before and after 1926. Does the strike fit into a larger pattern, or does it constitute an exception to the broad pattern of industrial relations between the wars?

KEY DATES

1919	Jan	Strike for 40-hour week in Glasgow.
	31 Jan	'Bloody Friday' – riot in George Square, Glasgow.
	Feb	Threat of strike by 'triple alliance'; Sankey Commission set up.
1920		Formation of Communist Party and of TUC General Council.
1921		8 million trade union members; 85 million working days lost in strikes.
	1 April	'day of decontrol' of the mines: national miners' strike began.
	15 April	'Black Friday': triple alliance collapsed.
	1 July	Defeated miners return to work.
1925		Only 8 million working days lost in strikes.
	31 July	'Red Friday': £23 million subsidy, Samuel Commission set up.
1926	11 March	Samuel Report published.
	30 April	Colliery owners began lock-out.
	3 May	Unofficial strike at *Daily Mail*; general strike began at 11.59 pm.
	5 May	Sir John Simon insisted the general strike was illegal.
	12 May	General Strike called off.
	13 May	Second, spontaneous strike.
	Dec	Last miners return to work.
1927		Trade Disputes Act.
1928		Mond–Turner talks began.

1 Post-war Crisis, 1918–21

KEY ISSUE Why was there a renewed outburst of strike activity?

The end of the war saw a return to traditional industrial procedures. The Restoration of Pre-war Practices Act of 1919 meant that women lost their places in industry to men, and at the same time 'dilution' ceased to be compulsory. Industrial courts, as set up during the war, still existed, but it was no longer obligatory to submit disputes for their judgement. Nor were joint industrial councils continued, except in the civil service. As a result, 1918–21 also saw a return to prewar industrial bitterness and confrontation. There was greater industrial conflict than in any previous period of British history.

After the war the trade union movement was stronger than ever before, with 8 million members in 1921 – about 48 per cent of the labour force, compared with only 20 per cent before the war. Allied with this strength went a mood of militancy, resulting in a new wave of strikes. In 1919 35 million working days were lost in disputes, and in the following year almost 27 million. The climax was reached in 1921 with a massive 85 million working days lost, twice as many as in the worst prewar year. Perhaps not surprisingly, the government began to fear that British workers might follow the example set in Russia, where the Communists under Lenin had seized power in 1917. The Prime Minister was told at the end of 1918 that there would be 'some sort of revolution' within the next 12 months. Another ominous sign was the formation of the Communist Party of Great Britain in 1920.

a) 'Red Clydeside'

After the war, British workers showed far less deference to their 'superiors'. Even the police went on strike in 1919, and it was feared that the army might refuse to obey orders, especially if called upon to act against British workers. The armed forces were put to the test on the Clyde, where the shop stewards' movement had been powerful during the war.

A strike for a 40-hour week began in Glasgow in January 1919, and the red flag was raised from the town hall. 70,000 workers stopped work, and a few days later – on 'Bloody Friday' – a riot began when police baton-charged a crowd in George Square. At a time when left-wing coups were being attempted in Germany and elsewhere, the government and Special Branch detectives took these events very seriously, and many spoke of a Bolshevik revolution. As a result, 12,000 troops armed with machine guns, together with 100 lorries and six tanks, were sent into Glasgow. They obeyed orders without question and the situation was soon calmed. But the leaders of the strike received only light prison sentences: neither the jury nor the judge at their trial believed that they had really been planning a revolution, and the head of Special Branch was accused of being unduly alarmist.

Despite the syndicalist rhetoric of many shop stewards, government fears of revolution were exaggerated. Most of the strikes were due to the rising cost of living. They were also unofficial rather than official stoppages, and soon trade union leaders began to regain control of their members. In 1920 the Trades Union Congress (TUC) – the 'parliament' of the trade union movement – was reformed. Previously it had been more an annual event than a permanent institution, but now it formed a General Council of about 30 members 'to co-ordinate industrial action'. However, this was not a sinister development, as some feared. The General Council was soon dominated by moderates like Walter Citrine, its first general secretary. Nor was the tendency of unions to amalgamate necessarily a dangerous sign. In 1922, for instance, 14 unions and around 300,000 workers united to form the Transport and General Workers' Union; but its founder, Ernest Bevin (see the Profile below), was another moderate who hoped to win better pay and conditions by reasoned argument rather than by confrontation.

ERNEST BEVIN (1881–1951)   *-Profile-*

Born in 1881 to the village midwife in the village of Winsford in Somerset, the youngest of seven children, Bevin knew real poverty in his youth and left school at the age of 11. He had several poorly paid jobs, and for 11 years, until the age of 29, drove a horse and cart delivering mineral water in Bristol. Then, in 1910, he organised the carters during a strike at the local docks. The following year he became a paid official of the dockers' union. His rise was then rapid. He became assistant general secretary of the union in 1920 and in 1922 he helped form the Transport and General Workers' Union.

A large man, who waddled rather than walked and whose hands resembled hams, Bevin seemed to his critics an unreasonable, belligerent character, bent on class war, wreckage and revolution. It was said in 1922 that no other trade union leader 'has assumed an attitude so truculent and irresponsible as Mr Bevin'. Yet in fact, while not averse to strikes, especially if they could be won, he also hoped to achieve his aims by negotiation and by imaginative appeals to public opinion. In 1920 he took the dockers' claim for a minimum wage of 16 shillings (80p) a day to an industrial tribunal. His opening speech lasted 11 hours and he showed, with complete mastery of the evidence, that dockers' pay had failed to keep pace with inflation and that the owners could afford to pay more. When experts pontificated about the number of calories a docker could live on, Bevin brought in actual plates of food to show how much – or rather how little – such figures really meant. To highlight the contrast in diet, he also produced a menu from the restaurant of the Savoy Hotel! The dockers won their case.

Bevin won a 44-hour week for the dockers but regularly worked 80 hours a week himself. He was a tireless and able administrator. It was he who gave some coherence to TUC organisation during the general strike, and, according to the *Sunday Express*, he was the only trade union leader 'whose reputation was enhanced' by the stoppage. After the strike he spearheaded union revival, he led the resistance of the Labour movement to cuts in benefits in 1931 (see page 127), and he campaigned in favour of rearmament in the late-1930s. His biographer, Alan Bullock, has described him as 'the outstanding trade-union leader yet produced by this, or perhaps any other, country'.

At the end of 1936 he experienced heart trouble, and he planned to retire soon. But instead he began a second career, as a politician. He was Minister of Labour in 1940–45 and Foreign Secretary 1945–51. He was one of the most important figures in Labour history in the twentieth century.

Similarly, many of the strikes of the period owed as much to the intransigence of employers as to worker militancy. Yet government fears were understandable since many workers voiced political as well as industrial demands. In May 1920 dockers refused to load a ship, the *Jolly George*, which they believed was to take weapons to the Poles in their war with communist Russia. This 'Hands off Russia' campaign achieved widespread support within the Labour movement. More significantly, miners were calling not just for higher wages or better conditions of work but for the nationalisation of the coal mines of Great Britain.

2 The Miners and 'Black Friday'

KEY ISSUES By what means was a general strike avoided in April 1921? What was the legacy of the union climbdown?

The government had taken control of the mines during the war in an attempt to prevent strikes and to maximise production, and most miners now wanted full-scale nationalisation. Only this, they believed, would lead to better and safer conditions of work and to the mechanisation of their technologically-backward industry. Already government control had brought about a national wages agreement – so that miners all over the country received the same wages for the same work – rather than the local agreements the owners favoured. In February 1919 the Miners' Federation called for wage rises and for nationalisation and, after a ballot of the members, threatened a strike. It seemed that they might be supported by the other two members of the 'triple alliance', the railwaymen and transport workers. The government then took action. There was at this time a shortage of coal in Europe, so prices were high and more miners than ever before were employed (1.25 million, about one-tenth of the entire British work force). A strike at this point would have been especially serious. The government therefore headed off a menacing confrontation by appointing a commission under the chairmanship of a judge, Sir John Sankey, to investigate and to make recommendations.

The evidence collected by the Sankey Commission created a sensation. It revealed the high profits made during the war, the scandalously low living conditions of many miners and their families (whose houses were 'a reproach to our civilisation'), and the chaotic and fragmented structure of the industry, with around 3,000 pits owned by 1,500 individuals or companies. There were also about 4,000 landowners to whom a royalty had to be paid for every ton of coal raised to the surface. The Commission made recommendations for wage rises and a shorter working day of seven rather than eight hours: both were accepted by the government. On the crucial issue of nationalisation the commissioners were deadlocked, and so Sankey had to use his casting vote. He cast it in favour of nationalisation, but the government refused to take action. The miners, in the words of one of their spokesmen, then felt 'deceived, betrayed, duped'.

The government was a coalition dominated by Conservatives, and to them nationalisation was anathema. The Prime Minister, Lloyd George, who was a Liberal, had little choice but to reject public ownership; and when the boom gave way to slump, so that the price of coal was halved and the industry began operating at a loss, he hastily handed the mines back to their owners. On the day of decontrol, 1 April 1921, a national miners' strike began. The owners tried to institute pay cuts, on local rather than national scales, but the men would have none of it. Lloyd George had skilfully delayed a strike until the postwar boom had given way to slump. By 1921 there was high unemployment and the edge was being taken off union militancy. Nevertheless, it seemed that the miners' action would escalate into a general strike, as the railwaymen and transport workers backed the miners.

All leave was stopped for members of the armed forces and the government declared a state of emergency. But Lloyd George was not resigned to a strike. On 14 April, Frank Hodges, secretary of the miners' union, in a meeting with ministers at the House of Commons, compromised by implying that the miners might be prepared to forego their insistence on national rates, at least for a time. The following day Lloyd George seized on this opportunity, inviting the miners' leaders to a meeting to discuss a temporary settlement. But the miners' executive, which had not authorised Hodges' statement, repudiated their secretary and refused to attend. Hodges was a reasonable man, Lloyd George a very slippery one. Perhaps the Prime Minister realised that his invitation would drive a wedge between the miners and that the other two members of the triple alliance, who were becoming increasingly reluctant to take action, would be provided by this disunity with an excuse to avoid action. This was certainly the outcome.

On 15 April 1921, soon to be known as 'Black Friday', J.H. Thomas of the railwaymen's union abruptly cancelled support for the miners, and the transport workers then did likewise. The 'triple alliance' had become the 'cripple alliance'. The miners went on strike alone and stayed out until 1 July, when they conceded defeat and returned to work on lower wages and with district agreements. They felt great bitterness towards their so-called allies. Thomas was, in his own words, subjected to 'abuse, calumny and misrepresentation'. In reality, the miners' two partners in the alliance had merely wanted to threaten a strike in order to get negotiations going: they had not actually wanted a strike. They knew that strike-breaking was much easier on the railways or in the docks than in the close-knit and often geographically isolated mining communities.

Union leaders did not forget 'Black Friday'. The miners decided that they could never again rely fully on other unions, while the leaders of the railwaymen and transport workers were determined that they should never again be considered traitors. The incident left deep scars and affected trade unions until a general strike did take place in 1926.

Nevertheless, industrial relations improved after 1921. The severe slump of 1921–2 made unions more reluctant to strike, and the number of working days lost because of industrial action declined steadily from 1922 until 1925, in which year stoppages accounted for fewer than 8 million days. The fact that inflation had given way to deflation added to this new climate. Unions did not have to demand higher wages for their members: a higher standard of living would be secured automatically if wage rates were not cut. As a result, most disputes were caused by management attempts to secure wage cuts, leading not to 'strikes' (in which workers withdrew their labour) but to 'lock-outs' (in which owners closed factory gates until workers would accept cuts in their pay). Even the mines saw better industrial relations, and in 1924 the owners agreed to wage rises. In addition, Stanley Baldwin, Prime Minister from 1924 to 1929, was a man of goodwill who had the sincere aim of promoting industrial peace. The omens for the future seemed bright.

3 The Origins of the General Strike

> **KEY ISSUES** How can we account for the mining dispute of 1926 and for the sympathetic action by the TUC which resulted in a general strike? What role did the government play in affairs?

a) Wages and Conditions in the Mining Industry

Higher wages were conceded by the owners in 1924, but circumstances then were exceptional. There was a shortage of coal on the world market, and thus British coal was in demand and commanded high prices. German coal was not available: the French had occupied the Ruhr in Germany in order to extract reparation payments in accordance with the Treaty of Versailles, and the Germans were responding with a campaign of passive resistance that effectively paralysed their coal industry. Strikes in the United States and Poland further enhanced the value of British coal. These conditions were unlikely to last long, and indeed in 1925 British coal again felt the full force of foreign competition. A new reparations deal with Germany, the Dawes Plan, meant that Germany paid her wartime debts by the export of free coal to France and Italy, whereupon demand for British coal plummeted.

Nor were working conditions in British mines improved in the early 1920s. They were as poor as ever. Amenities such as pit-head baths were in short supply, and safety precautions were appalling. A union official told the Sankey Commission that 'about four men are killed every 24 hours', and statistics collected between 1922 and 1924 largely bore out this statement. Over this three-year period 3,603 miners died and 597,193 were injured. These figures relate only to industrial accidents and do not take account of diseases, sometimes fatal, caused by the inhalation of coal dust over a long period. Anyone beginning work as a miner in 1920 would have a 2 per cent chance of being killed within the next 20 years, and a 50 per cent chance of being made seriously ill. Such casualty figures, which have been likened to those sustained in a war, are eloquent testimony explaining why industrial relations in the mining industry were so poor and why the industry was strike-prone. Mining was a hazardous occupation, and many believed that in view of the dangers they ran the miners should at least be able to earn a living wage.

b) 'Red Friday'

As the price of coal fell on the world market, so profits for British coal owners began to decline. This, in turn, led the owners to seek lower costs of production. In 1925 the industry was running at a loss, and at the end of June 1925 the owners insisted on wage cuts and longer hours. The men judged that they were being asked to take pay cuts of between 13 and 48 per cent, while at the same time the owners were to retain their traditional rate of profit – indeed profits were to be guaranteed regardless of the price of coal. The miners would not accept these terms, and neither would their two national union leaders.

The pliable Hodges had been replaced as secretary of the Miners' Federation by the fiery A.J. Cook, an ex-preacher who had been a syndicalist in the past (see page 42) and who was a member of the Communist Party. The Labour intellectual Beatrice Webb wrote that he was 'an inspired idiot' who became intoxicated with words when making a speech so that he scarcely knew what he had just said or was about to say next. The Federation's president, the Yorkshireman Herbert Smith, an orphan who had worked in the mines from the age of ten, was temperamentally very different. He was dour rather than emotional, a man of few words rather than a torrent. But both were incorruptible and devoted to the miners' cause.

The miners were prepared to fight alone. However, the General Council of the Trades Union Congress promised support, and a general strike once more seemed possible. Sympathetic action in support of the miners had failed to come about in April 1921, but TUC leaders had no wish to bear the stigma of another 'Black Friday'.

The government's reaction was to set up a court of inquiry under H.P. Macmillan. After their disillusioning experience with the Sankey Commission, the miners refused to co-operate; but the court nevertheless reported in their favour and against the owners, arguing that wages rather than profits should be the first charge on the industry. Baldwin saw representatives of the owners and of the unions separately but without achieving any breakthrough. Lower pay scales were to come into effect on 1 August 1925, at which time the TUC was to embargo the transportation of coal. Once more a general strike seemed almost certain.

Baldwin then acted. It can be argued that his government was in some degree responsible for the strike: by returning to the gold standard in April 1925, his Chancellor, Winston Churchill, had made

British exports more expensive and therefore less competitive abroad (see page 121). No responsibility was admitted or acknowledged, but even so Baldwin intervened on 31 July and granted a subsidy to the coal industry so that wages and hours could remain at their existing level for nine months, while profits of up to 13 per cent would also be subsidised. In the meantime, a royal commission was to report on the industry and make recommendations on its future. Baldwin had defied the right wing of his party, whose members thought it disgraceful that taxpayers should subsidise any industry: the Prime Minister was said to have given way to union intimidation. The Home Secretary, Sir William Joynson-Hicks, believed the whole issue would have to be 'fought out'. Was the country, he asked, to be governed by a parliament 'or by a handful of trade union leaders'? The *Daily Mail* called the subsidy a 'victory for violence'.

Some have said that Baldwin was cynically buying time, postponing the strike until his government was better equipped to defeat it. Yet this seems unlikely for several reasons. First, as Cabinet papers reveal, the government was fairly confident of beating a strike in 1925. Second, Baldwin had a sincere faith in the possibility of industrial harmony and was a man of genuine goodwill. He had once said, of the Taff Vale judgement: 'The Conservatives can't talk of class war: they started it'. A general strike was really the last thing he wanted. His government was busy during the nine months of the subsidy, revising and improving existing plans for coping with a national strike, but this was not so much cynicism as practical politics. While hoping for the best, Baldwin had to prepare for the worst.

As for the trade unions, they dubbed 31 July 'Red Friday'. Indeed some militants rejoiced in the belief that capitalism was failing: it almost seemed to them that a revolution was at hand. Most unionists thought that a great victory had been won. 'We have already beaten,' said Cook, 'not only the employers, but the strongest Government in modern times.' As a result of this optimism they made few preparations for a general strike, and so were at a decided disadvantage when one did occur.

c) The Samuel Report

Sir Herbert Samuel, a former Liberal home secretary, headed the royal commission. His report was ready in March 1926. It was a wide-ranging document and, though not calling for nationalisation, was highly critical of the whole mining industry. His recommendations contained much to displease the owners and to comfort the miners. He called for the provision of pit-head baths and of decent houses at new collieries, judged that wages should be agreed on a national basis, rather than local, and recommended that the working day should not be lengthened. This was currently seven hours, but working time began only when a miner reached the coalface, and this might be after walking or even crawling for a mile or two along narrow tunnels. (George Orwell, after personal experience, considered that 'this frightful business of crawling to and fro' was 'a hard day's work in itself'.) Samuel recommended that mining royalties should be nationalised, so that landowners would no longer receive profit for the coal mined by the companies, and called for the industry to be made more efficient by amalgamations. In addition, he wanted to see better retailing methods and more research into the uses to which coal could be put. Samuel believed that 'large progress' was possible along these lines, and he was adamant that no sacrifices should be required of the miners until the owners had agreed to adopt 'all practical means' for improving the organisation and efficiency of the industry.

Nevertheless, the report came to the conclusion that wage cuts were necessary in the short term. No precise level of reductions was specified, although Samuel implied that 10 per cent might be sufficient. Only such cuts, it was argued, could save the industry from disaster. The report was in many ways an even-handed document, containing something for each side in the dispute, but on the crucial issue of wage cuts it came down against the unions. The vital question was whether the parties involved would now accept the report as the basis for a settlement.

d) The Failure of Negotiations

Negotiations began at a very leisurely pace. Representatives of the owners and the miners met two weeks after the publication of the report, and immediately there was deadlock. The owners would not talk of reorganisation. Moreover they insisted on local as opposed to national wage agreements and still hankered after a longer working day. For their part, the union leaders would not accept wage cuts. Cook summed up the miners' position with the slogan 'not a penny off the pay, not a minute on the day'. Both Cook and Smith (whose most characteristic phrase was 'Nowt doin''') were poor negotiators, but the owners were also intransigent. There were some moderate and constructive owners, one of whom, Sir Alfred Mond, commented on the 'evil spirit' of his colleagues, but they were overshadowed by hard-liners. Lord Birkenhead, a cabinet minister, judged that he would describe the union leaders as 'the stupidest men in England' if he had not also met the owners!

But perhaps the government should also be criticised. While trying to get the two sides together, Baldwin refused either to renew the subsidy or even to make recommendations of his own. He was advised by one moderate owner to 'force' or 'impose' a settlement on the owners, but this he refused to do. The owners then attempted to end the deadlock by imposing their own terms – lower wages and a longer working day. When Smith and Cook rejected these terms, a lock-out began on Friday 30 April. The spectre of a general strike returned.

On 30 April 1926 almost 1,000 trade union representatives met in London and, after news reached them that the government had already proclaimed a state of emergency, they pledged support for the miners. Leading figures in the TUC had no positive wish for a strike: they tended to be much more moderate than Cook. This cleavage is best illustrated by the differences between Cook and J.H. Thomas, the railwaymen's leader and Labour MP. Cook was totally devoted to the miners' cause and had a contempt for the wealth of the capitalists. Thomas on the other hand, while retaining his proletarian image (so that he was said to drop his aitches as eagerly as he put on a dinner jacket), had acquired a taste for the 'good life' of high society. On the very day that Thomas was calling for 'a solution honourable and satisfactory to all sides', Cook was speaking of 'a war to the death'. Thomas warned his TUC colleagues that a general strike would lead to legislation against the unions and might indeed be a bloody affair in which their own lives would be in danger. Nevertheless the TUC felt that they must support the miners in their just cause.

It was agreed that a general strike should start at one minute to midnight on Monday 3 May. The miners' leaders then handed over 'the conduct of the dispute' to the General Council of the TUC and left London to help organise industrial action. Smith and Cook clearly believed at this stage that a general strike was inevitable; but in fact the TUC contacted the government again and began negotiating in earnest. The weekend was a very full and fraught one: ministers and TUC leaders had little sleep, so that tempers sometimes became frayed. At one time it seemed possible that the government would renew the subsidy for another fortnight in order for detailed negotiations to take place, but only on the precondition that the miners would agree in advance to accept some level of wage cuts. Miners' leaders were then recalled to the capital, but just as they returned the government broke off negotiations in the early hours of Monday 3 May. Baldwin had just heard that printers at the *Daily Mail* were refusing to work and, under pressure from the hard-liners in his Cabinet, decided that since industrial action had already begun further negotiations would be fruitless. TUC leaders were shocked, since they had neither authorised nor even known of the industrial action at the *Daily Mail*. Having investigated the issue, they returned to Downing Street but were told that the Prime Minister had gone to bed.

e) Could the Negotiations Have Succeeded?

No one can be certain whether negotiations could have averted a strike: this is a highly controversial issue which has attracted contrasting verdicts from historians. Yet it does seem that there were some grounds for a possible compromise. Cook was depicted in the press either as a dangerous revolutionary or as a short-sighted wishfulthinker unwilling to face economic reality (see the cartoons below and on page 98). But there is evidence that he saw the need to compromise. He told one of Baldwin's secretaries (and therefore the Prime Minister himself) that the miners' position was so weak that 'we shall have to have a national minimum not only with pluses above it, but minuses below it'. A more adroit man than Baldwin might well have exploited this sign of flexibility.

The other possibility was that the TUC might have been detached from the miners, as on 'Black Friday'. J.H. Thomas had grave doubts about the wisdom of a general strike. The *Daily Mail* incident was therefore of vital importance. Without it, the moderates in the TUC might have called off their support if the miners' leaders had refused to accept the principle of some level of pay cuts. Certainly when the

Cartoon from the *Daily Herald*, 28 July 1925

Cartoon from the *Daily Graphic*, 28 April 1926

TUC delegates were told that the government was no longer willing to negotiate, General Secretary Citrine was not alone in feeling 'that we had not been treated fairly'.

The printers at the *Mail* had refused to print an inflammatory editorial which branded the proposed general strike an attempt to destroy the government and subvert the rights and liberties of the people. Their action was spontaneous and was not authorised by either the TUC or the printers' union. It was certainly not the case that the TUC had broken their word and begun the strike early. The government side may therefore have used the action as an excuse to break off negotiations, and for this they should be criticised. It has even been suggested that the bellicose Winston Churchill, who had visited the offices of the *Daily Mail* earlier that day, might have arranged for the editorial to be written in the hope of provoking just such a reaction. The case against the Chancellor is not proven, but he certainly responded to the news with vigour: 'A great organ of the press is muzzled by strikers'. A colleague described him at this point as 'getting frantic with excitement and eagerness to begin the battle'.

f) Causes of the General Strike: an Overview

The strike had a remarkably long fuse, so that its origins can be traced back several generations. It may be seen as the culmination of a long history of bitter industrial relations in the mines, which in turn may be traced to poor working conditions, an appalling accident rate, and the failure of the owners to produce a coherent and efficient structure for the industry. Another mining dispute was nothing out of the ordinary and thus in a sense does not need explaining: the problems of the industry, exposed by successive reports but never rectified, meant that further industrial confrontation was only to be expected.

It is therefore important to distinguish between the causes of the mining dispute of 1926 and those of the sympathetic action authorised by the TUC. It was the latter which transformed yet another mining dispute into the unique General Strike. TUC action owed much to feelings of guilt about 'Black Friday' and to the widespread belief that, though economic realities demanded some reduction in wages, the owners were treating the men unfairly. Samuel later said that his commissioners never even contemplated such severe reductions in pay as the owners were seeking to impose. The TUC was also motivated by the need for solidarity in the face of the threat that, if miners' wages were reduced, general pay reductions for British workers might well follow. In 1925, during negotiations, Baldwin had said that 'all the workers of this country have got to take a reduction of wages to help put industry on its feet'. Self-interest thus seemed to unite all workers in a common struggle.

Nevertheless, the reluctance of the TUC to take action must be emphasised: they sincerely wanted to find a way to avoid confrontation, and ideally they wanted to achieve a solution by the threat rather than the reality of common action. In the end it was the government which gave them little choice but to go through with the first general strike in British history.

Responsibility for the strike must be shared between four groups: the miners' leaders, the TUC, the coal owners and the government. All these parties believed they were victims, but none can escape some share of the blame. Miners' leaders failed to convince their members that some wage cuts were necessary. The TUC representatives allowed themselves to drift into the position of entering a strike of which they disapproved. The colliery owners adopted an extreme position and refused compromise. Baldwin's government did little to bring the two sides together and called off negotiations when there was still a slight chance of averting the strike. The origins of the General Strike constitute a story with no heroes and with several parties contending for the role of villains.

4 The General Strike, 3–12 May 1926

> **KEY ISSUES** What was the relative strength of the two sides? What
> tactics did they pursue? Why did the strike last only nine days?
> Did it have important consequences for Britain?

a) The TUC and the Strike

Already one million miners were on strike (or, rather, were locked
out). Now, from one minute to midnight on Monday 3 May, the TUC
called out the railwaymen, dockers, road transport workers, printers,
and gas and electricity workers. Engineering and shipbuilding
workers were asked to strike a week later. In all, some 80 unions were
affected and about two and a half million men and women went on
strike, in addition to the miners. The response to the strike call was
not uniform throughout the country. Some seamen resolutely stayed
at work, and some parts of the countryside were little affected. But
what is really remarkable is the degree of worker solidarity that *was*
shown. For instance, even at the end of the strike well over 90 per cent
of railwaymen were solid in their refusal to work. There was very little
sign of a drift back to work as the strike proceeded. It was, in fact, the
most complete stoppage in Britain's history.

The TUC, however, did not call for a universal strike. Workers in the
health and sanitary services were excluded from the strike call, as were
those who transported food, although the government refused the
TUC's offer of maintaining food distribution. It was also hoped –
naively – that power workers, while cutting off the supply of heat, would
be able to maintain lighting. Nor was the term 'general strike', with its
syndicalist and revolutionary overtones, favoured by the TUC: instead,
they used the phrase 'national strike'. Having entered the strike very
reluctantly, the General Council was anxious to show that it was not revolutionary and that it was involved in an industrial rather than a political dispute. Hence it tried to pursue 'moderate' policies, especially by
attempting to minimise the inconvenience to the general public.

The General Council tried to make the strike appear as respectable
as possible. For this reason it declined a donation to the strike fund
of 2 million roubles (around £26,000) from Russian trade unions.
Citrine even went to the trouble of obtaining police permission
before sending half a dozen men to picket the offices of *The Times*,
and there was no attempt to use mass picketing or intimidation anywhere. Strikers were advised to stay at home, or to dig the garden,
rather than to go out on the streets. Approval was given to sporting
contests, and the TUC hoped that a football match at Plymouth
between strikers and the police (won by the former by two goals to
one) would symbolise the essentially moderate nature of the stoppage.

The TUC's direction of the strike was hindered by lack of effective preparations. Ernest Bevin was head of the strike organisation committee, and it was due to his administrative skills and hard work that some sort of coherence was improvised. Indeed, in view of the shortage of time to make preparations, we should probably conclude that the TUC machinery worked reasonably well. However, there was still a good deal of muddle. The local strike committees which were set up in towns and cities often received ambiguous instructions – or none at all – from TUC headquarters. Indeed the Swansea committee was so confused by contradictory messages that its members began to suspect that these constituted misinformation deliberately sent by the government. In this case the committee was wrong, but the government did intercept telegrams to and from the TUC and tap telephone lines.

Further research is needed before we may have a complete picture of the general strike in particular localities. So far there have been only a few dozen studies of local strike committees, out of the 465 that existed. Understandably these have focused on areas of particular local activity – such as Birmingham, Bradford and Doncaster – but the result is that our knowledge is patchy and that it is hard to generalise with confidence about the overall situation.

The main worry of the union leaders was that their inability fully to control the strike throughout the country might allow violence to erupt. The popular image that has survived of the General Strike is of its good-humoured holiday atmosphere. But this is a misleading half-truth. Certainly there were some worrying moments. Buses were overturned in Glasgow, police baton-charged crowds in Doncaster, and there were many other incidents, including some hand-to-hand fighting that looked as though it might turn vicious. (The novelist Arnold Bennett wrote in his diary on 5 May: 'General opinion that the fight would be short but violent. Bloodshed anticipated next week.') Nevertheless, such incidents were 'rumblings before a storm that never broke'.

Over 4,000 people were arrested and prosecuted (including prominent members of strike committees and about 2,000 members of the Communist Party of Great Britain), but given that the strike involved millions of people this figure is remarkably small. The longest prison sentence meted out was eight years, for someone who had helped derail an express train, the *Flying Scotsman*: the driver had in fact been stopped and warned that the rails had been pulled up, but he chose to drive on. Luckily no one was seriously injured in this incident. Nevertheless the TUC was anxious. Because authority was never fully in the hands of the General Council, it might pass to the local strike committees, which some called 'embryo soviets' on the Russian model. Certainly it seemed that the longer the strike went on, the greater was the likelihood that the TUC would lose control.

b) The Government and the Strike

While the TUC was anxious to appear moderate, the government was much more provocative. Almost its first action was to brand the strike a challenge to the constitution, rather than an attempt to stop the exploitation of the miners. This was the message printed in the government's newspaper, the *British Gazette*. Baldwin put Churchill in charge ('the cleverest thing I ever did: otherwise he'd have wanted to shoot someone'), and soon its circulation reached 2 million copies. There was no attempt at impartial journalism. Churchill said he could not be impartial 'as between the fire brigade and the fire'. He used the paper as a weapon in a propaganda war with the TUC, which replied with its own *British Worker*, edited by Hamilton Fyfe of the *Daily Herald*, its circulation reaching 0.5 million.

On 6 May the *Gazette* printed the following editorial:

1   The General Strike is in operation, expressing in no uncertain terms a direct challenge to ordered government. It would be futile to attempt to minimise the seriousness of such a challenge, constituting as it does an effort to force upon some 42,000,000 British citizens the
5   will of less than 4,000,000 others engaged in the vital services of the country.
    The strike is intended as a direct hold-up of the nation to ransom. It is for the nation to stand firm in its determination not to flinch. 'This moment,' as the Prime Minister pointed out in the House of Commons,
10 'has been chosen to challenge the existing Constitution of the country and to substitute the reign of force for that which now exists ... I do not think all the leaders who assented to order a general strike fully realised that they were threatening the basis of ordered government and coming nearer to proclaiming civil war than we have been for cen-
15 turies past'.

The following day came the response of the General Council of the TUC in the *British Worker*:

1   The General Council does not challenge the Constitution. It is not seeking to substitute unconstitutional government. Nor is it desirous of undermining our Parliamentary institutions. The sole aim of the Council is to secure for the miners a decent standard of life.
5   The Council is engaged in an Industrial Dispute ... Every instruction issued by the General Council is evidence of their determination to maintain the struggle strictly on the basis of an industrial dispute. They have ordered every member taking part to be exemplary in his conduct and not to give any cause for police interference. The
10 General Council struggled hard for peace. They are anxious that an honourable peace shall be secured as soon as possible. They are not attacking the Constitution. They are not fighting the community. They are defending the mine workers against the mine owners.

Many judged that Churchill won this war of propaganda, for however moderate the TUC leaders might be during the strike and however much they might protest that they were merely supporting the miners in a just cause, the fact was that their action was designed to coerce not the owners but the government. It was easy, therefore, to present the General Strike primarily as a contest between an elected government and a trade union organisation that did not represent the mass of the people. The fundamental issue tended to be seen as 'Under Which Flag?' (see the cartoon below).

UNDER WHICH FLAG ?

JOHN BULL. ' ONE OF THESE TWO FLAGS HAS GOT TO COME DOWN—AND IT WON'T
BE MINE.''

Punch cartoon, 12 May 1926

Churchill skilfully simplified the issues involved in the strike and called for the 'unconditional surrender' of the strikers. He also spread misleading information, insisting that strikers in particular parts of the country were returning to work when in fact they were not. Furthermore, when the government recruited a quarter of a million special constables (many armed with chair legs because regulation truncheons were in short supply), Churchill insisted provocatively that 'any action they may find it necessary to take' would have the full support of the government. The King himself found it necessary to complain about this, insisting that the law of the land should govern the conduct of all.

The government's plans, laid before the strike, worked well during it. The country had been divided into ten areas, each under a civil commissioner, and resources had been stockpiled. In February 1926 the Home Secretary had told the cabinet that 'little remained to be done' to prepare for the threatened strike. He also insisted that local authorities should not make poor relief available for strikers. As a result, essential services were maintained. Troops were used to man power stations, and there was no shortage of volunteers to help out. The government recruited men and women, and a private organisation, the 'Organisation for the Maintenance of Supplies', also put itself at the government's disposal. The unions believed that members of fascist organisations acted as volunteers and did their best to foment trouble. Certainly, several volunteers asked to be sent to Glasgow, where they could 'have a crack at them dirty Bolshies on the Clyde'.

Most volunteers, however, probably joined for the fun of novel work. Some fulfilled a lifetime's ambition to drive a train. Many undergraduates took part, the overwhelming number on the government's side, and members of the House of Lords were also eager to participate: three served as an engine-driver, a guard and a stationmaster. A former foreign secretary, Lord Grey, who was nearly blind, said he could not work as a special constable because he might hit the wrong man on the nose, but he was determined to unload ships. Society ladies played their part, and several posed for photographers as they peeled potatoes or cooked food in Hyde Park.

Yet such was the lack of expertise among the volunteers that many accidents occurred, especially on the railways, where four people were killed and at least 35 were injured. One man even contrived to drive a tram off its rails.

c) The End of the Strike

Baldwin broadcast to the nation on 8 May. He insisted that while he could not negotiate until the strike had been called off, he was nevertheless a man who was 'longing and working and praying for peace'. He asked to be trusted to 'secure even justice between man and man'.

On the same day, in sharp contrast, he and his Cabinet approved a bill that was to declare sympathetic strike action illegal, forbid picketing and make trade union funds liable for damages. It was decided that, unless the strike ended quickly, the bill would be pushed through Parliament in a single day. But there were signs that the legislation would not be needed. Certainly Baldwin's skilful words on the radio, confirming his reputation as a moderate, made a real appeal to the TUC.

By this time the General Council was beginning to regret calling the strike in the first place. There were few signs that worker solidarity was crumbling: indeed Bevin said that anyone suggesting in the East End of London that the strike should be ended 'would be in danger of his life'. But neither was there any sign that the strike would achieve an early victory. It looked as though it might be a long contest: and the longer it went on the greater were the chances that violence might flare up and the initiative pass to the revolutionaries. Several observers at this time independently drew parallels with the Russian Revolution, where the moderate Kerensky had been quickly replaced by Lenin.

The TUC was dismayed by an opinion voiced in Parliament on 5 May by the Liberal lawyer Sir John Simon that a general strike was already illegal – an incorrect verdict but one reiterated by a judge, Mr Justice Astbury, a few days later – and that therefore trade union assets might be seized. Thomas, the most reluctant member of the General Council to accept the strike in the first place, was the foremost voice in favour of ending it. He himself had organised several railway strikes in the past, but the longest had been of only ten days' duration. Acutely aware that, unlike the mines, railways were not 'blacklegproof', he insisted that the government was bound to win and that the longer the strike went on the more needless hardship would be caused. Thomas was therefore pleased when, on 8 May, he was contacted by Sir Herbert Samuel, who had recently returned from a holiday in Italy and put himself forward as mediator.

Samuel proposed a brief renewal of the subsidy, a return to work at the old rates of pay and then the resumption of negotiations to decide on reorganisation and wage reductions. Thomas seized on this initiative, even though Samuel made it quite clear that his proposals had not been accepted by the government. Joint talks were held on 10 and 11 May between Samuel, the General Council and the miners' leaders. Smith and Cook were not told that Samuel spoke without government approval, but even so there was no agreement. The TUC was for calling off the strike on the Samuel formula, but the miners were against. The miners, aggrieved that talks had started without their knowledge, would not agree in advance that wages should be cut. There was deadlock and an increasing bitterness between the TUC and the miners' leaders.

Walter Citrine's diary for 11 May is revealing of TUC thinking:

1   Reports came in from the country and showed that the men are as firm
as a rock. What then can be the cause of apprehension? I think it is
because most of us know that no matter how determined our men are
now, once the strike has reached its highest point and the maximum of
5 members have been called out, a gradual decline in economic power
must ensue. Then we shall have dribblings back to work here and there
… Our Council have quickly come to the view that they must make
their own decision in respect of policy … Herbert Smith is immovable.
Some of our Council members think he does not care who goes down.

The breach between the TUC and the miners was now seemingly
unbridgeable. Memories of 'Black Friday' no longer had much effect
on the General Council, one of whose members mused that 'Judas
Iscariot played a dramatic part in history. There could have been no
Jesus Christ without him'. Another said that they should 'no longer
grovel on our hands and knees before the miners'.

At 12.20 pm on Wednesday 12 May the General Council
announced the ending of their sympathetic action. The government
had made it clear to Samuel that his proposals were 'not clothed in
even a vestige of official character', and they were categorically determined not to resume the subsidy. The TUC had therefore surren-
dered unconditionally, even though they never admitted it to
themselves. Many strikers were joyful when they heard the news that
the strike was over – they assumed that they must have won. It therefore came as a bitter shock to realise that the TUC had capitulated.
The Communist Party described the calling off of the strike as 'the
greatest crime that has ever been committed'. Another observer
described the unions as 'an army of lions led by a few jackasses'.

TUC leaders had hoped that Baldwin would first use his influence to ensure that no returning strikers suffered victimisation from
employers, and would then help to solve the mining dispute on the
basis of Samuel's proposals. But they had obtained no assurances,
and in fact the Prime Minister did nothing of the kind. Some
returning strikers faced dismissal and many more faced reduced
wages. The result was that, on 13 May, a second – and spontaneous
– strike began in protest. Indeed it is probable that more people
refused to work after the strike had been called off than during the
nine days of the official strike. Most employers then became more
flexible, but even so it is probable that many thousands were vic-
timised in some way as a result of their support for the General
Strike.

As for the miners, they reaped no benefit from the massive sympathetic action launched by the TUC. Chancellor of the Exchequer
Winston Churchill tried hard to achieve a settlement, and to force the
owners to compromise, but without success. The miners stayed on
strike until the end of the year but finally had to admit total defeat –
reduced wages, longer hours and local wage agreements. Even their

unity was damaged, as a breakaway 'non-political' union was formed in Nottinghamshire.

d) Why the Strike Failed

The General Strike, literally a 'nine days' wonder', achieved greater support from workers and their families than even optimistic union leaders had predicted. A cabinet minister wrote in his diary that 'immense numbers of workers' had come out against their will and were 'longing to go back', but were afraid to do so because of fear that their families would be bullied. However, there is little evidence to support this view. The strike exhibited remarkable worker solidarity and cannot be said to have collapsed. So why did it fail?

One important factor was that the government had planned well for the strike. The civil servant who masterminded its plans, Sir John Anderson, had done so with remarkable thoroughness. 'Before the computer was perfected,' it has been said, 'Anderson was a tolerable substitute'. In sharp contrast, the unions had failed to plan at all for the strike. After 'Red Friday', they had judged the battle already won. A.J. Cook, for instance, merely advised his mother-in-law to buy an extra tin of salmon each week – drawing from J.H. Thomas the caustic comment 'By God! A British revolution based on a tin of salmon'.

Another vital factor in the failure of the strike was the readiness of people to act as 'patriotic volunteers' (from the point of view of the government) or 'strike breakers and blacklegs' (from the standpoint of the unions). The railways were virtually paralysed, despite the efforts of the volunteers, but road transport functioned relatively smoothly and prevented the strike from having maximum impact. In earlier decades, before the proliferation of motor vehicles, the strike would have been much more effective.

These factors meant that the strike could not succeed in the short term – a crucial fact, since the TUC were banking on a quick victory. The General Council were not revolutionaries: they were responsible and moderate men, anxious that the strides made by trade unionists over the previous decades should not be destroyed. They were reluctant to take sympathetic action in the first place and had no wish to see the strike produce bitter and violent confrontation.

The TUC leaders were caught in a logical dilemma which, in the end, almost guaranteed their defeat. They authorised strike action to support the miners in their battle to prevent a 'savage deterioration' in their living conditions. In this sense the strike was an industrial dispute. However, their sympathetic action was designed to coerce not the mine owners but the government, and as a result politicians were able to present the action as a challenge to the constitution. In this sense the General Strike *was* political. In the resulting battle of words, which put the unions on the defensive, the miners' cause was pushed into the background. Perhaps the TUC would have done better not to call out the printers, since by this action it allowed the government, through control of the *British Gazette* and the BBC, to achieve a stranglehold over the media which the improvised *British Worker* could do little to loosen. Soon it seemed to the TUC that they had everything to lose from the strike and nothing to gain. At this stage Samuel's intervention provided them with a convenient pretext to call off an action which, all along, their heads had told them was unwise.

The TUC leaders have been heavily criticised. They have been called timid men who mistrusted their supporters more than their opponents and who feared the consequences of victory more than those of defeat. They were not 'consciously traitorous', one historian has written, 'but they lacked moral fibre'. Thomas, in particular, has been the butt of criticism: there were 'mules and fools' among the strike leaders, it has been said, but only one traitor. On the other hand, it can be argued that the General Council's reasoning was correct: the strike was not being won, union funds were being exhausted in strike pay, and sooner or later violence might have spread. Much depends on the hypothetical issue of what would have occurred had the strike continued; but it is at least arguable that the TUC were acting sensibly in calling it off. Perhaps if the miners' representatives had been more shrewd then they too would have ended the strike on 12 May. Certainly they achieved absolutely nothing by staying out for another seven months, and pitiful reports of hardship in mining communities – with women about to give birth without adequate food, clothing or bedding – show the price they paid.

The miners had been able to call on the TUC as their allies, but this escalation of the dispute enabled the mine owners to call on the government. It was an unequal contest. The General Strike failed because the TUC was opposed by the resolute power of the government and of the State. Baldwin, stiffened by his right wing, could not allow the strike to succeed. Detachments of the British army were stationed outside many of the major cities. Their use was not authorised, but it would have been had the situation deteriorated. The State could also call on vast financial resources. The nine-month coal subsidy, which Baldwin had been so reluctant to renew, totalled £23 million; but in the nine days of the strike the government spent a total of £433 million. In contrast the trade unions spent £4 million and could afford no more.

e) Significance of the Strike

How should the General Strike be interpreted? There are two basic issues – what the strike tells us about industrial relations between 1919 and 1926, and its effects on the future.

One school of thought emphasises that the strike was really about class warfare. According to this interpretation, leaders on the left had long been dreaming of a general strike to bring about a fundamental shift in political power, while capitalists and right-wing politicians such as Churchill and Joynson-Hicks had long been aiming to crush the trade union movement and reassert the power of property-owners. This antagonism came to a head in 1926. There is some truth in this analysis: the events of 1926 reveal much class solidarity – for instance, the volunteers were almost all middle-class – together with hostility between the classes, and certainly there were leading figures on both left and right with extreme and belligerent attitudes. The problem with this line of argument is that such men were less important in 1926 than is often imagined. Cook had certainly been a syndicalist in his earlier years, but his biographer has shown that by 1926 he was no longer a revolutionary: he wished merely to defend the miners' position and was far from optimistic about the outcome. In the end, he simply bowed to the wishes of the majority of miners. On the government side, Baldwin did much to tame his right wing, and even Churchill, who was so provocative during the strike, proved remarkably conciliatory after it. Nor did employers conform to type: they reduced wages in the wake of the strike less markedly than they had in the period before it (perhaps a sign that the strike was not altogether a failure).

It seems fair to conclude, therefore, that the General Strike was not the result only of class antagonism but also of specific problems and, to some degree, of the mistakes and miscalculations of individuals. It is not difficult to imagine that, had the adroit Lloyd George rather than the stolid Stanley Baldwin been Prime Minister, a general strike might well have been averted.

Nor was the General Strike necessarily the climax of industrial bitterness in the period after the First World War. It can be argued that 1919–21 saw the height of militancy, with a crop of unofficial strikes, political demands from Labour and a record number of working days lost. 1922–5, a period of relatively high unemployment, saw a lessening of industrial conflict and fewer days lost. The events of 1926 were perhaps merely an exception to the broad trend of better industrial relations.

What of the effects of the General Strike? Was the strike a turning point? Such a dramatic event as Britain's first and (so far) only General Strike must, it is assumed, have had clear-cut and momentous consequences. The commonest interpretation is that the strike was both an end and a beginning – an end to the old romantic notions of syndicalism and direct action and the beginning of a new mood which stressed moderation and collaboration in trade union affairs. Historians generally have a liking for clear-cut interpretations, but sometimes historical reality is so complex as to defy such simple analysis. There was admittedly a trend towards moderation after 1926, but under men like Bevin and Thomas this had been apparent even earlier, and the General Strike was not the only factor making for collaboration between capital and labour. High unemployment levels after 1926, and in particular during the depression of 1929–32, were also important. Nor should it be supposed that no one on the left henceforth hankered after revolution. The General Strike was seen by some hard-liners as a magnificent demonstration of working-class power that would have achieved victory but for its betrayal by spineless TUC leaders. 'The response of the workers was beyond all praise', wrote the *Workers' Weekly*, but 'the leadership was beyond contempt'. The mystique of a general strike had thus not been entirely destroyed. There was both change and continuity after 1926.

5 Industrial Relations, 1927–39

> **KEY ISSUE** How different were industrial relations in this period, compared with 1918–26?

a) The Trade Disputes Act, 1927

After the General Strike, Baldwin found it impossible to resist calls from right-wingers for a change in the law. The Trade Disputes Act was the result. It made any strike illegal that was 'designed or calculated to coerce the Government either directly or by inflicting hardship upon the community'. There could be no repetition of May 1926. Strike activity had to be confined to the 'trade or industry in which the strikers are engaged'. Illegal 'intimidation' during strikes was defined more widely than ever before. Finally, the Act insisted that henceforth trade unionists who wanted to pay the political levy to the Labour Party would have to make a point of 'contracting in'. Before this all unionists had paid unless they deliberately 'contracted out'. Because of the apathy of many workers, who had not troubled to contract out before 1927 and did not trouble to contract in afterwards, Labour Party funds soon declined significantly; but if the government hoped to weaken the links between Labour and the unions it signally failed. The unions now rallied behind Labour, as they had done after Taff Vale, in an effort to secure change through Parliament and especially to get the 1927 Act repealed.

b) The Mond–Turner Talks

There was a good deal of bitterness from rank and file union members towards their leaders after May 1926, but it soon subsided. Almost all the leaders of 1926 were re-elected to their offices. Most union members decided that the whole episode of the General Strike – and not just its ending – had been a mistake. A new temper in industrial relations gradually became apparent.

In 1928 and 1929 a series of meetings took place between employers and the TUC. These talks were named after Sir Alfred Mond, a moderate coal-owner and the creator of Imperial Chemical Industries, and Ben Turner, Chairman of the TUC. But the two key individuals were Mond and Ernest Bevin, both of whom believed that employers and workers should co-operate out of enlightened self-interest. Cook, disgusted at this dialogue with the industrial enemy, cast scorn on 'Mond Moonshine', and it must be admitted that little of practical benefit emerged from the talks. A joint report recommended changes in industry to the benefit of both employers and workers – and especially regular consultations between management and unions in each industry – but the depression beginning in 1929 provided poor circumstances for the implementation of reforms. The talks may have helped the General Council to recover some prestige after the General Strike, but on the whole they symbolised the new industrial atmosphere rather than achieved concrete improvements in industrial relations.

c) Effects of the Great Depression

The Great Depression lasted from 1929 to 1932. Unemployment peaked at 3 million, but even after this period parts of British industry were heavily depressed. As a consequence, union membership – and therefore union revenue – declined. Membership totals fell from a maximum of over 8 million in 1921 to a low point of 4.4 million (less than one-third of all wage earners) in 1934. Even so, these figures should be seen in perspective. The blows trade unionism suffered put the clock back, but only to the position of 1914. Union membership at its lowest point in the 1930s was still four times the size of that in 1888, and from 1934 onwards there was expansion. In 1939 just over 6 million workers were in trade unions.

During the depression industrial relations were undoubtedly strained. Collaboration between unions had been dealt a blow by the General Strike, but even so national strikes took place in the textile industry in 1929, 1930, 1931 and 1932. Nevertheless conditions did not favour strikers – too many firms were going bankrupt and too many unemployed workers were willing to act as strike-breakers – and the decade has been described as one of 'sullen industrial peace'. Indeed between 1927 and 1939 the average annual total of working days lost was just over 3 million, compared with 28 million between 1919 and 1925. In 1934, for instance, fewer working days (a mere 959,000) were lost in strikes than in any year since 1900. Rather than take the offensive, most union leaders simply tried to minimise wage-cutting. Even the mines were relatively peaceful. Smith retired as president of the miners' union in 1930 and Cook died the following year. They were replaced by more moderate figures.

Ernest Bevin was the key figure in this period. He worked extremely well with Walter Citrine, the General Secretary of the TUC, even though the two men were of contrasting temperaments and indeed disliked each other. It has been said that they formed 'one of the most successful involuntary partnerships in modern politics'. Under their leadership, the TUC became much stronger than ever before. The 'Bridlington Agreement' of 1939 enabled the TUC to settle disputes between unions and laid down precise regulations to govern union competition and to prevent the poaching of members. The General Council also assumed the power to expel offending unions.

Trade unions had become much more politically minded than ever before, and much more constructive. Even Conservative politicians now listened to what the unions had to say, and in 1937 Bevin claimed that the unions were an integral part of the State. Certainly their officials found numerous positions on governmental advisory committees and commissions. But, despite this, his claim was premature. It was during the Second World War, as in the war of 1914–18, that the unions were taken into partnership with government. By 1940, when Bevin became Minister of Labour and National Service, history had indeed come full circle, and the General Strike had been forgotten by all but a few.

Summary Diagram
The General Strike and Industrial Relations Between the Wars

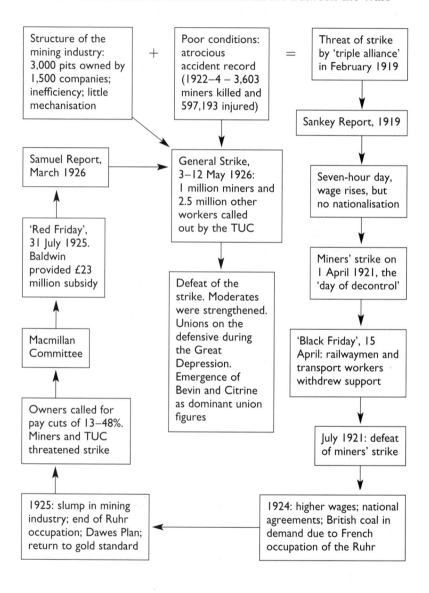

```
┌─────────────────┐     ┌─────────────────┐     ┌─────────────────┐
│ Structure of the│     │ Poor conditions:│     │ Threat of strike│
│ mining industry:│  +  │ atrocious       │  =  │ by 'triple      │
│ 3,000 pits owned│     │ accident record │     │ alliance'       │
│ by 1,500        │     │ (1922–4 – 3,603 │     │ in February 1919│
│ companies;      │     │ miners killed   │     └─────────────────┘
│ inefficiency;   │     │ and 597,193     │              │
│ little          │     │ injured)        │              ▼
│ mechanisation   │     └─────────────────┘     ┌─────────────────┐
└─────────────────┘              │              │ Sankey Report,  │
                                 │              │ 1919            │
┌─────────────────┐              ▼              └─────────────────┘
│ Samuel Report,  │──▶ ┌─────────────────┐              │
│ March 1926      │    │ General Strike, │              ▼
└─────────────────┘    │ 3–12 May 1926:  │     ┌─────────────────┐
         ▲             │ 1 million miners│     │ Seven-hour day, │
         │             │ and 2.5 million │     │ wage rises, but │
┌─────────────────┐    │ other workers   │     │ no nationalisation│
│ 'Red Friday',   │    │ called out by   │     └─────────────────┘
│ 31 July 1925.   │    │ the TUC         │              │
│ Baldwin provided│    └─────────────────┘              ▼
│ £23 million     │             │              ┌─────────────────┐
│ subsidy         │             ▼              │ Miners' strike  │
└─────────────────┘    ┌─────────────────┐     │ on 1 April 1921,│
         ▲             │ Defeat of the   │     │ the 'day of     │
         │             │ strike.         │     │ decontrol'      │
┌─────────────────┐    │ Moderates were  │     └─────────────────┘
│ Macmillan       │    │ strengthened.   │              │
│ Committee       │    │ Unions on the   │              ▼
└─────────────────┘    │ defensive during│     ┌─────────────────┐
         ▲             │ the Great       │     │ 'Black Friday', │
         │             │ Depression.     │     │ 15 April:       │
┌─────────────────┐    │ Emergence of    │     │ railwaymen and  │
│ Owners called   │    │ Bevin and       │     │ transport       │
│ for pay cuts of │    │ Citrine as      │     │ workers         │
│ 13–48%. Miners  │    │ dominant union  │     │ withdrew support│
│ and TUC         │    │ figures         │     └─────────────────┘
│ threatened      │    └─────────────────┘              │
│ strike          │                                     ▼
└─────────────────┘                          ┌─────────────────┐
         ▲                                   │ July 1921:      │
         │                                   │ defeat of       │
         │                                   │ miners' strike  │
┌─────────────────┐                          └─────────────────┘
│ 1925: slump in  │                                   │
│ mining industry;│    ┌─────────────────┐            ▼
│ end of Ruhr     │◀───│ 1924: higher    │
│ occupation;     │    │ wages; national │
│ Dawes Plan;     │    │ agreements;     │
│ return to gold  │    │ British coal in │
│ standard        │    │ demand due to   │
└─────────────────┘    │ French          │
                       │ occupation of   │
                       │ the Ruhr        │
                       └─────────────────┘
```

Working on Chapter 5

Pay particular attention to the causes of the General Strike and the reasons for its failure. Make a real effort to sympathise with, and then to criticise, the four main groups involved with these events – the mine-owners, the government, the miners' leaders and the TUC – before reaching a final verdict. Do you think that the TUC was right to call off the strike when they did?

Answering structured and essay questions on Chapter 5

Consider the following structured question:

a) What factors led to so many strikes in Britain in the period 1919–21?
b) Why were there fewer strikes in 1922–25?

Essay questions on the General Strike are common. They can either single out the strike itself or consider it as part of a longer time-span.

1. Discuss the view that the General Strike was doomed to failure from the start.
2. Why did the General Strike fail and what were the consequences of this failure for the future?
3. Why were industrial relations issues so important in British politics between 1918 and 1927?

Construct both first and final paragraphs for all three questions, being careful to avoid repetition. Remember that while at the start of an essay you may outline an argument, in the conclusion you must be much more precise. For instance, for the third question, while you might in the first paragraph voice various possible explanations for the import-ance of industrial relations issues, by the final paragraph you should be much more definite, perhaps by highlighting the most important factor.

Alternatively, questions can focus on a longer period of time. For example:

4. What factors affected the development of the trade union movement between 1914 and 1927?
5. How powerful was the trade union movement between 1918 and 1939?

Source based questions on Chapter 5

1. Cartoons of A.J. Cook

Study the cartoons on pages 97 and 98, from the *Daily Herald* and the *Daily Graphic*. Answer the following questions:

a) The *Herald* cartoon is dated 28 July 1925 and the *Graphic* cartoon 28 April 1926. What events prompted them? Explain which depiction you think more accurately reflects Cook's role in those events. (*6 marks*)
b) Comment on the way the *Herald's* cartoonist has drawn Cook. Is he being criticised or praised? Justify your answer. (*4 marks*)

c) Comment on the way the cartoonist has drawn Cook in the *Graphic*. What impression of him would the reader gain? (*5 marks*)

2. Newspapers during the General Strike

Read the extracts from the *British Gazette* and the *British Worker* on page 102. Answer the following questions:

a) Churchill insisted in the *Gazette* that four million strikers were challenging 42 million citizens. Given that Britain's total population was around 46 million, can these figures be justified? Explain your answer. (*3 marks*)

b) Was Churchill justified in calling the strike 'a direct hold-up of the nation to ransom' (line 7 in the *Gazette*)? Explain your answer. (*4 marks*)

c) Baldwin had a reputation for being a moderate. How far is this reputation borne out by his statement to the House of Commons (lines 8–15 in the *Gazette*)? (*3 marks*)

d) What, in practical terms, do you think the author of the *British Worker* extract meant by i) 'a decent standard of life [for the miners]' (lines 4–5), and ii) 'an honourable peace' (line 11)? (*4 marks*)

e) Are there any signs in the extract from the *British Worker* that the TUC's willingness to continue the strike was faltering? Support your answer with quotations from the extract. (*3 marks*)

f) Compare and contrast the two extracts as pieces of propaganda. (*8 marks*)

g) Use your knowledge to judge how far these two extracts adequately sum up the aims of the two sides during the strike. (*10 marks*)

6 Governments and the Economy

POINTS TO CONSIDER

We have seen that Britain's economy in the interwar years suffered several slumps, and an especially severe depression in 1929–31. This chapters examines the response of governments. You need to be aware of what actions the politicians took, and you should also understand the 'economic model' which underlay their actions. At the same time you need to be aware of the alternative strategies put forward by Maynard Keynes and to judge how viable they were.

KEY DATES

1925	**April**	Return to the gold standard (£1 = $4.86); Keynes responded with *The Economic Consequences of Mr Churchill*.
1929		Colonial Development Act.
1931	**July**	May Report (calling for 10% cut in dole), leading to a 'run on the pound'.
	23 August	Labour cabinet split over expenditure cuts.
	24 August	MacDonald formed the National Government: 10% cut in dole and other benefits soon instituted.
	15 Sept	the 'Invergordon Mutiny'.
	21 Sept	Britain went off gold standard.
1932		Import Duties Act.
	August	Ottawa economic conference.
1934		Special Areas Act.
1935		Keynes's *General Theory*.
1937		Special Areas (Amendment) Act.

1 The Treasury View and the Return to Gold, 1918–25

KEY ISSUES What problems faced the British economy after the First World War? Why did Britain return to the gold standard in 1925?

a) Post-war Boom and Bust, 1918–22

Lloyd George won a general election at the end of 1918 with a promise to create 'homes fit for heroes'. There was a general expectation that governments would intervene much more actively in the economy than before the war in order to promote the welfare of British citizens. The Minister of Reconstruction voiced a widely-held view in 1918 when he said that the war through which the country had passed 'has enlarged its sense of what is possible, and at the same time quickened its sense of what is fair and right'. The economy had been mobilised for war and now, it seemed, it would be mobilised to ensure higher standards of living in peacetime.

Before the war Lloyd George had introduced old age pensions and national insurance against sickness and unemployment. Now he extended the insurance system to include allowances for dependants of the unemployed and 'uncovenanted' benefit ('the dole') for those whose insurance had expired. He also began an ambitious house-building programme. As during the war, he showed a bold willingness to improvise and innovate. In 1921 he chose Sir Robert Horne, the candidate he described as the 'least wedded to financial orthodoxy', as his Chancellor of the Exchequer. Yet in the circumstances of 1921, when the postwar boom ended (see page 59), not even the new Chancellor could resist traditional policies. Lloyd George's coalition was dependent on the support of the Conservative Party, and Tory MPs insisted that since government revenue was falling – with fewer people in work and so able to pay tax – government expenditure should be cut back. In 1922 the 'Geddes' Axe', wielded by a Tory minister, pruned expenditure by over 10 per cent. Here was an end to the government's radical policies. The last wartime controls were removed and the housing programme was abandoned.

The British economy was beset with 'structural unemployment' (see page 60). Perhaps new policies were needed, especially a regional policy to help the 'depressed areas'. But instead the Treasury tried to return to the past, to the policies pursued during the 'golden age' of the nineteenth century.

b) The Treasury View and Orthodox Economics

Treasury thinking derived from the so-called 'classical' school of economics which had grown up in the late eighteenth century. According to this viewpoint, the 'law of supply and demand' determined the workings of the economy. The demand for goods would always be about equal to the supply because of the operation of the price mechanism. Those with goods to sell would find a market at a price satisfactory to both buyer and seller. This was also true of those who sold their labour as workers. Similarly, those who wanted to lend money and those who wanted to borrow would, in the end, agree on a rate of interest acceptable to each party. Indeed the whole economy would naturally be in a state of balance or 'equilibrium'.

According to this theory, there might be economic crises, but the price mechanism of the market would ensure they were short-lived. If, for instance, changes in the tastes of consumers meant that a certain article was no longer popular, then either the cost of the article would be lowered until it began to sell again or, eventually, the workers employed in manufacturing it would be thrown out of work. If the latter happened then, according to the classical economists, this should be readily accepted: there was no point in people working to produce what consumers did not want to buy. The result of redundancy would be a pool of cheap labour available to supply the real needs of the public. Thus unemployment would be merely temporary: it would cure itself because people out of a job would be willing to work for lower-than-average wages and would thus soon find employment. If the whole of the economy went into recession, this too would, in the end, cure itself. In a slump prices would fall until people started consuming again, and in addition interest rates would fall until capitalists again found it profitable to borrow money and expand the economy.

Classical economists thus believed that the economy was self-correcting. Prosperity was natural, and slump and unemployment were unnatural and temporary aberrations. All was for the best in the best of all possible worlds – so long, that is, as governments followed a policy of *laissez-faire*, standing aside and allowing individuals to follow their own economic self-interest. If governments intervened too much, then the law of supply and demand would break down and the 'market economy' would cease to function.

The First World War had been a profound shock to orthodox economists. Victory in the war could not be left to natural market forces. The government could not stand aside: instead it had had to intervene and insist on the production of vital war materials, while at the same time increasing taxation and borrowing to pay for escalating expenditure. It was all very distressing to the supporters of orthodox economics. Now, after the war and after the onset of the slump, they could return to 'sound finance'.

After the war civil servants at the Treasury had four main aims, which some have judged were held so tenaciously as to constitute dogma rather than reasoned judgements.

i) They wanted to see the budget balanced. The orthodox view was that no government should spend more than it raised in revenue through taxation. If a budget was unbalanced, government would have to borrow to pay for expenditure not covered by taxation, and this, it was thought, would have harmful consequences. The more demand there was to borrow, the higher interest rates would be – and high interest rates would deter businessmen from borrowing and investing for future growth. In addition, the more government borrowed, the less would be available for businessmen to borrow; and since governments would not use loans as constructively as private capitalists, an unbalanced budget would thus have harmful effects on the whole economy. Furthermore, most economists believed that 'expenditure' should include not merely spending on social services but the repayment of wartime debts or, at the very least, payment of interest on these debts. Otherwise the country would have to raise new loans to pay off old ones and would never be free of an escalating burden of debt. (Interest service charges reached 20 per cent of government expenditure after the war.)

ii) It was also thought desirable that a government should balance its budget at a low level of income and expenditure. The more government spent on services, the more it would have to tax the nation; and the more income was taken by taxation, the less would be available for individuals to spend. If, because of heavy taxation, the demand for goods fell short of supply, then production would have to be cut back until equilibrium was reached once again. In short, government taxation interfered with the law of supply and demand. According to this view, governments could best help the economy by practising economy and refusing to spend above a bare minimum on administration, defence and social services.

iii) Another canon of economic orthodoxy was a belief in free trade: goods should be allowed freely to enter Britain from abroad, without the imposition of tariffs. It was thought that if Britain pursued free trade, then other countries would be more likely to follow this enlightened example, and the result would be the largest and most profitable market for British exports. In addition, it was believed that healthy competition from foreign imports would stimulate the modernisation of British industry.

iv) Finally, the Treasury was convinced that the value of the British currency, the pound sterling, should be maintained and that, if possible, there should be fixed exchange rates amongst the world's leading industrial nations, so as to facilitate international trade. These objectives, the civil servants believed, would lead to the return of business confidence and so to British prosperity. The means of achieving them was a return to the gold standard.

c) The Gold Standard

Civil servants believed that they should take a 'long view' of the economy: short-term political manoeuvres – while beloved of politicians-in-search-of-votes at election time – were not in the real interests of the nation. They therefore wanted a policy which one official described as 'politician-proof' and another more candidly called 'knave-proof'. The gold standard had provided such a policy.

d) The Return to Gold, 1925

The 'Treasury View' proved remarkably influential in the 1920s. Successive chancellors were careful to balance the budget and to avoid borrowing. It was said of the teetotaller Philip Snowden (the Labour Chancellor in 1924 and 1929–31) that he would 'no more

THE GOLD STANDARD

The gold standard was the means by which, before the First World War, the world's leading industrial nations had ensured financial stability. A country on the gold standard fixed the value of its currency in terms of a set amount of gold, so that there were 'fixed' as opposed to variable or 'floating' exchange rates between currencies. In addition, the money supply (the amount of notes in circulation) depended on a country's gold reserves, and so a government could not simply print as many notes as it chose and cause inflation.

This system had provided for international financial stability in the nineteenth century and had minimised the degree to which governments interfered in the economy. Like the classical economic model, the gold standard was self-regulating. Problems would sort themselves out.

If, for instance, a country had a large balance of payments problem through importing more than it was exporting, then, under the rules of the system, gold would have to be exported to pay for the excess. This would automatically produce a reduction in the volume of currency in circulation, which in turn would produce a fall in the price of goods produced at home. Additionally, if gold was leaving the country interest rates would rise to discourage investors from switching their investments into other currencies and causing a 'run' on the local currency. These higher interest rates would then make credit more expensive and leave less money available for the purchase of goods, which would fall in price. With lower domestic prices, exports would be cheaper – and so the balance of payments problem would be overcome. The gold standard thus seemed the perfect mechanism for ensuring stability and prosperity.

have dreamt of budgeting for a deficit than of going into a public house'. The Conservative Chancellor from 1924 to 1929, Winston Churchill (who in fact drank a lot!) also believed that government expenditure was an evil, albeit sometimes a necessary one. Churchill's view was contained in the phrase 'Let the money fructify [be fruitful] in the pockets of the people'. Free trade was also accepted as orthodoxy for most of the decade. Industrialists who wanted protection against foreign imports were defeated.

The keystone of orthodox policy was the gold standard. During the war, when expenditure far exceeded gold reserves, the system could not operate effectively, and in 1919 Britain formally 'went off gold'. Since then problems for the British economy had multiplied.

In particular, around a million men (10 per cent of the insured workforce) were regularly unemployed. The economy was refusing to obey the laws of classical economics. Unemployment should have corrected itself: the price mechanism should have led to more jobs, though at lower wages than before. What had gone wrong? Perhaps economic theory needed to be modified to take account of new realities. Yet most economists believed the main problem to be the absence of the gold standard. In the prewar period, when this system had operated, Britain had been relatively stronger economically: sterling had been the most dominant international currency and the City of London had acted as banker to most of the world. Now the dollar and New York were more powerful. Hence in April 1925 the Treasury and the City persuaded Churchill to return Britain to the gold standard in the hope that prewar prosperity would also return.

Equally significantly, they persuaded him to return at the 'prewar parity'. This meant that the pound was valued at its prewar level of 4.86 dollars. Churchill had been unsure about the return to gold at this fixed exchange rate. He once said that his advisers might just as well have been speaking in 'Persian' for all he understood of their complicated jargon. But in the end he consoled himself with the thought that the Governor of the Bank of England, Montagu Norman, and the leading Treasury officials must know more about these complex matters than 'anyone else in the world'. Treasury experts were certain that, in the long run, the gold standard would benefit the British economy. Politicians would have less power to interfere, and manufacturers for export would have the benefits of a fixed exchange rate: their goods would cost a set amount abroad, instead of varying as the pound rose or fell in relation to other currencies.

Admittedly the pound was now being given a higher exchange rate, so that at a stroke British goods would cost more abroad, but other countries were expected to follow Britain's example and return to the gold standard at their prewar parities. In the meantime, higher export costs, it was thought, would have benefits. High wages were adding to the price of British goods and making the economy uncompetitive. Now, under the stimulus of a strong pound, employers would be forced to cut wages and become more efficient. A general round of wage cuts, it was hoped, would make British industry more competitive. Such cuts would lead to falls in the price of goods at home as well as abroad. In other words, wage reductions would not lead to cuts in the *standard* of living, for the *cost* of living would fall proportionately with wage reductions. The return to the gold standard would be an economic panacea. All would soon be well, or so it was hoped.

2 The Keynesian Alternative

> **KEY ISSUE** How did Keynes's economic views differ from those of the establishment?

a) Keynes and the Return to Gold

One economist – John Maynard Keynes (see the Profile below) – considered these Treasury arguments to be 'of the feather-brained order'. Indeed he thought that the return to the gold standard at the prewar parity was a positive disaster. He argued that the pound was being over-valued by about 10 per cent and that the attempt to cut wages by a similar amount would produce needless industrial strife, followed by wage cuts and unemployment. He predicted that the coal industry would soon be the scene of confrontation.

> 1 Our export industries are suffering because they are the first to be asked to accept the 10 per cent reduction. If everyone was accepting a similar reduction at the same time, the cost of living would fall, so that the lower money wage would represent nearly the same real wage as
> 5 before. But, in fact, there is no machinery for effecting a simultaneous reduction. Deliberately to raise the value of sterling money in England means, therefore, engaging in a struggle with each separate group in turn, with no prospect that the final result will be fair, and no guarantee that the stronger groups will not gain at the expense of the weaker
> 10 ... On grounds of social justice, no case can be made out for reducing the wages of the miners ... The plight of the coal miners is the first, but not – unless we are very lucky – the last, of the Economic Consequences of Mr Churchill.

The attempt of the colliery owners to reduce wages in June 1925 – soon to result in the General Strike – goes far to justify Keynes's interpretation of the return to the gold standard. Most historians now see the return to gold at the prewar parity as an important cause of the industrial strife of 1925–6. Even Churchill later admitted that he had made the 'biggest blunder' of his life. Nevertheless the significance of the return to gold has been disputed. One writer has called the return 'the most dramatically disastrous error by a government in modern economic history', and another has called the miners a 'human sacrifice' to gold. But to some historians such judgements are grossly exaggerated. They insist that in reality the pound was revalued in April 1925 by less than 10 per cent and that, since British exports were uncompetitive anyway, their new, higher price had little practical effect. At least the uncertainty associated with a floating pound had disappeared, with a consequent boost to business confidence. Also, import prices were lower, so home consumers gained. One cautious historian has concluded that the return to the gold standard was of no more than 'marginal significance in Britain's economic difficulties'.

JOHN MAYNARD KEYNES (1883–1946)

-*Profile*-

Keynes was the brilliant son of a wealthy Cambridge family, an aesthete and something of a philosopher as well as an economist. In 1919 he had attacked the Treaty of Versailles in his brilliant book *The Economic Consequences of the Peace*. Then, in 1925, he produced a pamphlet, *The Economic Consequences of Mr Churchill.*

Keynes was an unusual economist. Most academic economists were interested in theory, in economic models, and had a rather detached view of the real world. In general, they were wedded to the idea that economic problems would sort themselves out in the long run so long as governments practised *laissez-faire*. Keynes, on the other hand, had a highly developed social conscience: he believed that economics should serve social ends. He therefore mocked the traditional view that, in time, problems like unemployment would sort themselves out. 'In the long run,' he retorted, 'we are all dead'. To his mind, progress and prosperity were far from inevitable and he called for governments to intervene energetically in order to minimise hardships and promote prosperity.

Keynes was in some ways an anti-theorist. In the 1920s he believed that all theories were inadequate because in the real world, as opposed to textbooks, there was always a large measure of uncertainty about economics. What was needed therefore was to face problems with the confidence that human ingenuity could find a solution. The German Chancellor Bismarck had once said that politics was 'the capacity of always choosing, in constantly changing situations, the least harmful, the most useful'. Keynes advocated such an approach for economics, and he was therefore a severe critic of the rigid Treasury outlook.

His views were fully expressed in his *General Theory of Employment, Interest and Money* (1936), where he argued that employment was dependent on the total ('aggregate') demand in the economy – and that government could, if necessary, supply that demand. Gradually he converted the establishment to his way of thinking, and he was an adviser to British government during and just after the Second World War, when he helped to create the International Monetary Fund and the World Bank.

Economic developments after April 1925 did not justify the return to gold. Other countries, including France and Belgium, followed Britain's example, but they returned at new parities. Certainly there was no return to Britain's nineteenth-century economic dominance, and nor could there have been since the basic causes of that dominance no longer existed. The Treasury had short-sightedly mistaken the symbol of British prosperity (the gold standard) for its root cause. As a result the British economy was handicapped: not only were exchange rates relatively high but interest rates had also to be kept high in order to protect the pound's fixed valuation. Under the gold standard regime, sterling could be freely converted into other currencies; and to prevent investors – some would say speculators – from switching from pounds to other currencies or to gold and producing a 'run on the pound', the Bank of England had to make it attractive for them to keep their investments in sterling by keeping interest rates – and thus the return on their investment – relatively high.

b) Keynesian Theory

By 1929 Keynes was convinced that governments should intervene energetically in the economy, for instance by beginning large-scale public works to provide jobs. To orthodox economists this proposition made no sense: it would involve borrowing money, and such money would merely be diverted from capitalist entrepreneurs to the government. Hence jobs created by public works would be matched by jobs lost as a direct result elsewhere in the economy. Keynes disagreed. He admitted that savings (that is, that proportion of people's income not spent on consumption) might be inelastic, but he argued that not all savings were currently being invested. Many people had money in current accounts – 'on deposit' – in the banks, rather than properly invested. There was therefore a surplus of savings which could be tapped, and in his view government should do the tapping, borrowing the surplus savings and creating the jobs which so many people needed.

3 The Great Depression, 1929–32

KEY ISSUES What policies were used by governments in this period to combat the depression? Were there alternatives?

a) The 1929 Election

Keynes not only opposed the Treasury view but also challenged politicians to act decisively to tackle the country's economic problems. The first to respond were Lloyd George and the Liberal Party. In the

1929 election Lloyd George stood on a manifesto called 'We Can Conquer Unemployment', aiming to reduce unemployment to 'normal proportions' within a year by an extensive scheme of public works. Keynes endorsed this programme. The other two parties, Labour and Conservative, stuck to traditional policies. Labour called for 'socialism', without having any real idea of how to achieve it. The Conservatives, the party in government, campaigned on the slogan 'safety first'.

Churchill insisted that 'We should not try to compete with Lloyd George but take our stand on sound finance'. Conservatives took their lead from the Treasury, members of which defaced a copy of the Liberal manifesto with the words 'Extravagance, Inflation, Bankruptcy'. The Treasury continued to insist that governments could not safely create large numbers of extra jobs, as money to promote public works could either be borrowed, in which case it would be diverted from investment elsewhere and tend to push up interest rates, thus stifling economic growth; or it could be raised from taxation, and so reduce consumer spending and produce unemployment; or it could be printed, at the cost of inflation.

The Liberals improved their vote at the election but did not achieve power. Some believed that a golden opportunity had been lost to cure Britain's economic ills (see the cartoon on page 126). Labour won the largest number of seats, although without an overall majority, and formed the second Labour government. In effect the election saw a victory for 'economic conservatism' against 'economic radicalism', for both the Conservatives and Labour favoured traditional Treasury views. Keynes remarked that Snowden, the first supposedly socialist chancellor, was also the 'last adherent of true blue *laissez-faire*'.

b) Labour's Policies in the Depression

Labour had the difficult task of grappling with the Great Depression from October 1929. Unemployment mounted towards 3 million and foreign trade slumped alarmingly. J.H. Thomas, the new Minister for Employment, later wrote that 'I was facing a world economic blizzard that no man or government could cope with'. Many commentators also believed that there was no solution to these problems: after all, the depression was worldwide, and no country coped noticeably better than Britain in 1929–32.

The Treasury and the Bank of England believed that the situation would eventually improve by itself, and meanwhile government should observe the canons of sound finance, balancing the budget and encouraging workers to accept wage levels that would not result in their pricing themselves out of work. Above all, official advice was that the government should not indulge in financial gambles that would probably only make a bad situation worse. In addition, public

'The lifeboat that stayed ashore', David Low cartoon, the *Evening Standard*

works on a large scale would be impossible to organise in the short term, a view with which Herbert Morrison, Labour's Minister of Transport and an administrator of experience and skill, fully agreed. As a result, the government did not attempt to provide a large number of jobs by this method. Although expenditure on public works doubled from £70 million in February to £140 million in September 1930, this was insufficient even to prevent the unemployment totals from continuing to rise.

Another token effort was made at the end of 1929, when the Colonial Development Act made £1 million a year available to promote development schemes in the British Empire. The aim was not so much to develop the colonies as to create jobs in Britain: it was hoped that the Act would create extra orders for British industry and so absorb unemployment. But the sums involved were so small, and grants to the colonies were hedged around with so many restrictions, that the effects of the scheme were negligible.

The Treasury's main advice was that the budget had to be balanced. This was very hard to achieve, for while government revenue from taxation was falling as more people became unemployed, the cost of unemployment benefit was escalating, from £12 million in 1928 to £125 million in 1931. Snowden wished to follow orthodox advice to scale down expenditure in general and the level of unemployment benefit in particular – in other words, to deflate the economy. But such cuts would be very unpopular with the bulk of the Labour Party, which regarded itself as the party of the underdog and the unemployed. The Chancellor therefore pursued a policy of 'drift'. No thorough or consistent policy was followed: instead the budget was left unbalanced for as long as possible.

Crisis came in 1931. A large deficit in the balance of payments was announced, while bank failures in Europe meant the loss of British investments. The pressure for Labour to balance its budget increased, especially when a royal commission on unemployment insurance called for reductions of up to 30 per cent in unemployment benefit. A month later, in July, the all-party May Commission painted a gloomy picture of the country's economic prospects, predicting a £120 million budget deficit for the coming year unless a 20 per cent cut was made in unemployment benefit. Traditional economists believed that unemployment benefit was preventing the economy from returning to equilibrium: men would not work for reduced wages when they had the 'dole' to fall back on. A cut might therefore put the economy back on its feet.

Snowden, backed by Prime Minister Ramsay MacDonald, insisted that cuts in expenditure ('retrenchment') should replace drift. To make matters worse, a 'run on the pound' began: after the gloomy May Report foreign investors, fearing that Britain faced bankruptcy, began to withdraw funds in alarming quantities. By the end of July 1931 almost a quarter of the Bank of England's gold reserves had been used up. Snowden was convinced of the need to borrow money from international bankers to maintain the gold standard. He told the Cabinet that the loan was absolutely vital but that bankers in New York and Paris would only consent to lend the money if, first, expenditure was cut and the budget balanced.

Would a Labour Cabinet take the unpopular action of cutting unemployment benefit? In the summer of 1931 ministers were recalled from their holidays for key Cabinet meetings. But instead of decision there was deadlock. A group of ministers led by the Foreign Secretary, Arthur Henderson, would not accept cuts for the unemployed, and Ernest Bevin led a delegation from the Trades Union Congress (described by one irate minister as 'pigs') to lend its considerable weight to this resistance to cuts. The Cabinet split 12–9 in favour of a package of reductions totalling £78 million, including a 10 per cent cut in unemployment benefit. Snowden later complained that a large number of his colleagues 'tamely submitted to the intimidation' of the TUC.

The division in the Cabinet meant that MacDonald and Snowden were unable to secure acceptance for their proposals. Instead, on 24 August, they joined with Conservatives and Liberals in a coalition. The National Government was born.

c) The Alternatives to Orthodoxy, 1929–31

The Labour government had done little to tackle the Great Depression. They had avoided taking firm action, and when they could no longer drift along they had left office. It has been said that their socialism was impractical. Labour ministers could conjure up an appealing vision of a future socialist society of justice and harmony, and equally they could denounce the evils and inequalities of capitalism. But they could not offer coherent policies to bring about the transition from capitalism to socialism. However, the key question is whether the government could have done better. Were there other options open to them, besides the financial orthodoxy of the Treasury and the Bank of England?

The answer must be that there were. In 1930 the Prime Minister made former union leader J.H. Thomas head of a small ministerial team to tackle unemployment. The group included a wealthy 33-year old convert from the Conservative Party, Sir Oswald Mosley, and it was he who produced a memorandum of alternative proposals. Mosley wished to see protective tariffs to restrict imports, a greater use of credit to provide public works and promote expansion, more government direction of industry to promote rationalisation and efficiency, and increased pensions and allowances to boost domestic consumption and encourage earlier retirement. Borrowing ideas from Keynes, Lloyd George and the Conservative protectionists, he produced a positive package of proposals. However, his ideas were rejected by the Cabinet. Philip Snowden was firmly against such unorthodox ideas; the Prime Minister backed up the Chancellor; and Thomas – who got on very badly with his young assistant – also opposed the reforms. As a result, Mosley left the Labour Party and, despairing of democracy's capacity to achieve positive economic results, formed a fascist organisation (see *Britain: Domestic Politics, 1918–39* in this series for further details).

After the rejection of the Mosley Memorandum, MacDonald himself took responsibility for unemployment policy. The Prime Minister had never specialised in economic affairs and was in many ways out of his depth. He set up commissions and committees to investigate aspects of Britain's economic woes, but this was done merely to buy time. While the issues were being investigated, the government would survive – and possibly the depression might end by itself. Nevertheless MacDonald did receive advice which contrasted with Treasury thinking. There were two main sources for this. One was a 15-man Economic Advisory Council (a sort of economic 'think tank') and the other was the Committee on Finance and Industry, presided over by a judge, Lord Macmillan. Keynes was a prominent member of both of these bodies, and he was the main source of alternative economic ideas. An important confrontation took place when the Macmillan Committee questioned the Governor of the Bank of England.

Montagu Norman made a bad showing: later he admitted that he had not even understood some of Keynes's questions. When asked on what theoretical basis he formed his judgements, the Governor simply tapped his nose and kept silent! By now Keynes had strengthened his own theoretical ideas. In particular he began to develop what later became known as the 'multiplier effect', the idea that once people were set to work prosperity would be generated throughout the economy. New workers would also be consumers, and to supply their needs more men would be taken on who, in their turn, would become consumers, and so on – and on and on. Public works would have a valuable knock-on effect, but they could not be started unless the government agreed to finance them and so 'prime the pump'. Keynes was also becoming increasingly critical of the government's policy of high interest rates. These were needed to safeguard the gold standard, but at the same time they were stifling domestic investment. Even a member of the Bank of England admitted that high interest rates, while meeting their target, had unfortunate side-effects: they were 'a blunderbuss not a rifle'.

Keynes used two key words to summarise the differences between his views and those of the orthodox establishment – 'enterprise' and 'thrift'. The Treasury view was based on 'thrift', and this was a misguided policy because to cut benefits and wages in a depression would simply lower purchasing power and thereby reduce consumption and so throw more people out of work. For this reason Keynes called the May Report 'the most foolish document I ever had the misfortune to read'. His own view was based on 'enterprise', and this led him to be attracted to a whole host of unorthodox proposals. In his own words, he 'twisted and turned to try to find some aid to the situation'. He favoured tariffs against foreign imports, so that domestic industry would be protected during the depression, and also recommended the use of large-scale public works. In fact, he told MacDonald that he was 'in favour of practically all the remedies which have been suggested'. He added that a negative attitude – 'the repelling of each of these remedies in turn' – was to his mind the only unforgivable sin.

In the crisis of August 1931, as the Cabinet was reaching deadlock over cuts in expenditure, Keynes recommended a further policy – that Britain abandon the gold standard. Snowden was insisting that Britain faced bankruptcy: there was a 'run on the pound' and Britain needed to borrow money from abroad, a precondition for which was a balanced budget. But, reasoned Keynes, this financial crisis was really artificial. If the pound were not tied to gold and to a fixed exchange rate, there would be no emergency. The pound would 'float' and find a realistic exchange rate, and furthermore Britain's domestic budget could be framed without regard to the wishes of overseas bankers. Moreover, Britain would then have control over its own interest rates, without the need to maintain the fixed exchange rate of sterling. In short, Keynes wished to see the sort of flexible response to the depression which the rigid gold standard system made impossible. But his advice was ignored.

Most figures on the left refused to countenance cuts in unemployment benefit from an instinctive, 'gut reaction' feeling that there had to be a better way to solve the country's problems than by inflicting hardship on people who were already the victims of capitalism. But not all who opposed the Treasury view did so for emotional reasons alone. Trade union leader Ernest Bevin had been a member of both the Economic Advisory Council and the Macmillan Committee, where he formed a close alliance with Keynes, and under his guidance TUC views were far more progressive than those of the Labour government. We can thus see quite clearly that alternative policies were open to MacDonald and his ministers. Yet they do not seem to have seriously considered them.

d) The Suspension of the Gold Standard

The National Government was formed on 24 August 1931 to take the action at which Labour had baulked. The new Cabinet, containing Labour, Conservative and Liberal ministers, was committed to economic orthodoxy. Philip Snowden, who continued as Chancellor, made economies of £70 million in government expenditure, including a 10 per cent cut in unemployment benefit. He also increased taxation, lifting the standard rate of income tax from 22 to 25 per cent. These measures balanced the budget and allowed the government to negotiate a loan from abroad. Even so, to the surprise of ministers and the horror of Montagu Norman, Britain was soon forced off the gold standard.

Snowden's search for economies led him to cut the salaries and wages of government employees, and on 15 September British sailors in the fleet at Invergordon protested by refusing to obey orders. News of the 'Invergordon mutiny' produced a flight from sterling. This renewed 'run on the pound' depleted the country's gold reserves to such an extent that the Governor of the Bank of England decided that the gold standard would have to be suspended. Many people expected dire consequences to follow, including rapid inflation, and the pound fell from $4.86 to around $3.40. But it was soon realised that this 30 per cent devaluation was largely beneficial: it resulted in a more realistic exchange rate and it cushioned Britain from the effects of financial speculators. Several former Labour ministers were amazed at what had happened. 'Nobody told us we could do this', complained one. In fact Keynes and Bevin had actually advised the Prime Minister to do precisely this.

Soon most people realised that the gold standard had been a 'sacred cow' which had needlessly complicated Britain's economic problems. It had been a mistake to return to gold at the prewar parity in 1925 and foolish to retain the standard for so long. One element of dogma had been removed from financial thinking. Would the government henceforth play a more constructive role in the economy?

4 The Years of Recovery, 1932–9

> **KEY ISSUES** What part did government play in Britain's recovery from the Great Depression? Did it remain true to the traditional Treasury view or did it show a willingness to adopt Keynesian techniques?

Keynes's ideas were changing, and it was not easy to keep up with them. In 1936 his *General Theory of Employment, Interest and Money* was published. This was his most important publication – he believed it would over the next ten years 'largely revolutionise … the way the world thinks about economic problems' – but also one of his least accessible to the non-expert. Its basic idea was that the level of employment depended on the total of 'aggregate demand' in the economy – in other words, the total amount of spending (consumption and investment), whether by individuals or government. It followed from this that the government could, by spending enough, determine levels of employment, and this is exactly what Keynes urged should be done. Instead of simply balancing the budget by matching expenditure to income, government should manage the economy by influencing levels of aggregate demand. Put crudely, governments could generate full employment if they spent enough.

There were signs during the 1930s that politicians, taking their lead from Treasury officials, were becoming more open-minded. For instance, they were less opposed than hitherto to public works: indeed during the 1935 election campaign the Chancellor announced a five-year road-building programme costing £100 million. One expert, seeing the influence of Keynesian thinking in this scheme, has noted that 'the pillars of sound finance were no longer set in stone'. Nevertheless the pillars still existed. Many traditional views remained, alongside some new ideas. It is probably true to say that official economic policy was modified but not transformed.

a) The National Government's Economic Strategy

After the round of expenditure cuts and the ending of the gold standard in 1931, there were several noteworthy features to the government's economic strategy. The policy to which the government gave most prominence was unorthodox: a system of protection was introduced.

At the end of 1931 stop-gap measures were taken: the government was given the power to impose import duties at short notice on goods that were entering the country in 'abnormal' quantities. But early the following year the Import Duties Act imposed a general duty of 10 per cent on all goods entering Britain, although goods from the British Empire were to be exempt, pending an imperial conference to be held in Ottawa later in the year. Many hoped that the Empire would become a self-supporting economic unit, enjoying free trade amongst its members while protected by tariff barriers against the rest of the world. But the conference proved disappointing. Dominions like Canada and Australia feared that if the Empire were free-trading, their own infant industries would suffer too much competition from British manufactured goods. As a result, they would not remove tariffs against British goods. Instead, they simply raised tariffs against non-British foreign items. Hence a measure of preference was given to imperial goods, but not an effective one. While it is true that during the rest of the 1930s Britain traded more than ever before with the Empire (so that exports to the Empire increased from 36 to 46 per cent of total trade between 1931 and 1938, and imports from the Empire over the same period rose from 25 to 38 per cent), the overall level of trade was not boosted. Most historians therefore agree that Britain's new tariff policy had little real effect on economic recovery.

More important were policies to which the government gave less attention. First, realising the benefits of a 'weaker' pound – in particular that exports were cheaper and therefore more competitive – the government took deliberate action through the Exchange Equalisation Fund to keep the value of the pound down, selling sterling when it looked likely to rise in value. This policy may have been of benefit to the economy, but its significance should not be exaggerated. After all, the recovery was essentially in industries producing for domestic consumption rather than for export (see page 69). Secondly, the government, no longer constrained by the gold standard, instituted a policy of low interest rates. Interest rates were lowered from six per cent in 1931 to two per cent the following year and were kept at this level until 1939.

Keynes approved both these aspects of government policy: they encouraged 'enterprise' rather than 'thrift'. But in fact the government also fostered an economic climate which discouraged borrowing and therefore probably hindered recovery. At the Exchequer Neville Chamberlain, Chancellor from 1931 to 1937, was a cautious man who, like his predecessors, believed in the importance of balanced budgets. He urged people to 'tighten their belts' rather than spend. In his budget speech in 1932 he recommended 'hard work, strict economy, firm courage and unfailing patience' to the nation. The following year his message again comprised the same puritanical prescription. At the very time when Britain was emerging from the depression – because of the upturn in the trade cycle, the housing boom and the growth of expenditure on consumer goods (see pages 69–70) – the government was discouraging expansion. 'Aggregate demand' (to use Keynes's phrase) was growing, but it was fuelled by private rather than public spending.

b) The National Government's 'Unemployment Policy'

'Cyclical' unemployment disappeared as the 1930s wore on, but 'structural' unemployment remained at high levels (see page 65). The staple industries of coal, textiles, iron and steel, and shipbuilding remained depressed in the 1930s as they had been in the 1920s. The National Government made only a token effort directly to cure unemployment and to help the depressed areas. In 1934 the Special Areas Act made £2 million available in aid. As a result, about 44,000 workers were encouraged to move to other towns and another 30,000 were found places on retraining courses. Some improved social amenities, such as parks and swimming pools, were also provided. But the sums involved were small, areas like Lancashire (which Lancastrians judged to be a depressed area) were not included in the scope of the Act, and nothing substantial was achieved. The two unpaid commissioners who were responsible for implementing the legislation criticised its limitations and resigned in 1936. One of them insisted in his last report that 'We must not fear making a break with the traditions and practices of the past'.

Public criticisms led the government to pass the Special Areas (Amendment) Act in 1937. This tried to encourage firms to establish factories in the distressed areas by offering remission of rates, rent and income tax, up to 100 per cent for five years. But again little of substance was achieved. New trading estates were set up in South Wales, the North-East of England and in Scotland, but they employed hundreds rather than thousands. The Lord Mayor of Newcastle described it all as 'a mere flea-bite and a sop'. What really provided work in such areas was rearmament, and the unemployment problem was only really cured by the Second World War.

The Special Areas Acts produced cosmetic changes, and were designed to do no more. The government's low-key approach was a reflection of its general economic philosophy. It had decided not to attack the problem of unemployment directly. Its philosophy was summed up by Neville Chamberlain in 1935

> **The quickest and most effective contribution which any Government can make towards an increase of employment is to create conditions which will encourage and facilitate improvement in ordinary trade.**

Despite tariffs and a managed exchange rate, the government remained true to the traditional notion that its essential task was to allow market mechanisms to function: in this way financial stability would encourage business confidence. It therefore had no 'employment policy' as such. Governments had a responsibility to relieve the poverty that stemmed from unemployment rather than to create jobs.

5 Conclusion: Governments and the Economy

KEY ISSUE Should governments be praised or blamed for rejecting Keynesian alternatives to Treasury orthodoxy?

Just as Britain's economic performance in the interwar years has been the subject of contrasting verdicts, so has the role of governments in the economy. Governments have been praised for a good job well done and have also been condemned for woeful inadequacy. It is generally acknowledged that they made mistakes: the return to the gold standard at the prewar parity was perhaps the most obvious. Furthermore, most experts on the interwar years have concluded that politicians – including some chancellors – were out of their economic depth. They simply did not understand economic and financial mechanisms. But defenders insist that there were successes as well, the inauguration of the Central Electricity Board in 1926 (see page 62) being one of the clearest examples. They also point out that Treasury policy became more flexible (especially as the 1930s wore on) and more willing to plan for economic growth.

The key issue is whether – especially during the Great Depression – governments ignored viable solutions to Britain's problems. Would a more positive, Keynesian thrust have produced greater economic success? In particular, would mass unemployment have been cured or at least alleviated? If so, then governments should rightly be condemned for tolerating such high levels of unemployment and for accepting levels of economic growth far below the optimum of which the British economy was capable.

a) Did Keynes Have the Answers?

The response to this question has varied over several decades. Until the early 1970s, it was generally believed that Keynes had undoubtedly been right. Keynes became an economic adviser to the Treasury in 1940, and his thinking then dominated economic strategy. Britain experienced high levels of employment from 1940 until the late 1960s: this was the 'age of Keynes', and it was assumed that never again would Britain have to tolerate mass unemployment. During this period the record of the interwar years, and particularly the 1930s, seemed especially poor. Governments had ignored the realistic policies which Keynes had presented to them. Hence politicians were the 'guilty men' who had sacrificed a generation of working people on the altar of Treasury dogma. No criticism seemed too harsh for them, and no praise too great for Lord Keynes.

During the 1970s, however, economists became divided, and many if not most began to see fatal flaws in Keynes's theories. The world was now in the 'post-Keynesian age'. In particular it was said that Keynes's ideas produced inflation. His emphasis on 'demand' produced not greater 'supply' but price rises – and such inflation could only be cured by higher interest rates and, ultimately, by the very unemployment his policies were designed to eliminate. As Keynes had previously been excessively praised, so now he was excessively condemned as an essentially arrogant man whose social concerns had led him to misjudge what was feasible in the real world. Many economists decided that the orthodox views of the interwar period had been correct: governments should stand aside and let businessmen produce jobs and prosperity. Several historians have now reinterpreted 1918–39 to show that the Treasury, while making some mistakes, had been broadly correct to insist on balanced budgets and 'sound finance' – and to be wary of Keynes's 'solutions'.

The issue is confusing to non-experts. Perhaps the most acceptable view lies somewhere between the extremes. Keynes had exposed the rigidities in Treasury thinking between the wars, especially the naive view that the economy would return to 'equilibrium' at full employment if left alone. It made little sense to continue to look upon unemployment as a temporary aberration that would cure itself when over a million men were continuously out of work for well over a decade. On the other hand, Keynes did not have all the answers, and he probably failed to take sufficient account of business confidence. Indeed it may well be true, as John Ramsden has argued, that had Keynes's views been applied in the circumstances of July 1931 their sheer novelty and the abhorrence with which most bankers and businessmen viewed them might well have led to economic collapse. Furthermore, while the stimulation of 'aggregate demand' might well have led to economic expansion, there was no guarantee that this would not have produced even greater growth in the South East while leaving the depressed areas still depressed. Keynes's other main idea – government-sponsored public works – would not have revived the ailing staple industries and might well have created administrative difficulties that would have diminished their impact. In short, Keynesian thinking was much more relevant to 'cyclical' than to 'structural' unemployment.

b) Assessment

Governments between the wars, with the exception of the Lloyd George coalition in 1918–20, followed cautious policies. 'Safety first' was their watchword. Probably they were over-cautious; and it is probably true to say that their policies neither helped nor hindered the economy to any great extent. The politicians may have settled for this verdict. On the whole they were fearful men – but it must be admitted that there was much to be fearful of. There was runaway hyperinflation in Germany in the early 1920s; the collapse of banks in 1929–32; and mass discontent leading to political upheaval and even revolution in several European countries. In Britain, traditional policies sacrificed the possibility of economic revival to minimise the possibility of economic collapse.

Perhaps politicians were wrong to be so cautious, but it is hard to blame them for not throwing in their lot with untried and untested policies. They received an enormous amount of advice and, while it was conflicting, most of it was in favour of orthodoxy. Keynes was not quite a 'voice in the wilderness', especially from 1932 onwards, but he was always in a minority.

Keynes had made a fortune on the stock market by 1936, but he had earlier lost a fortune in 1921. Had he converted governments to his ideas, Britain might have undergone economic revival and transformation between the wars. The 'Hungry Thirties' might never have existed. On the other hand, there might have been collapse and disaster: the very real improvements in British industry and in the standard of living experienced by most people in the 1930s might never have materialised. No one can really be sure what the results would have been had different polices been pursued, although it is fascinating for historians and economists to speculate. Politicians, however, felt they had to be circumspect in dealing with national finances.

Summary Diagram
Governments and the Economy

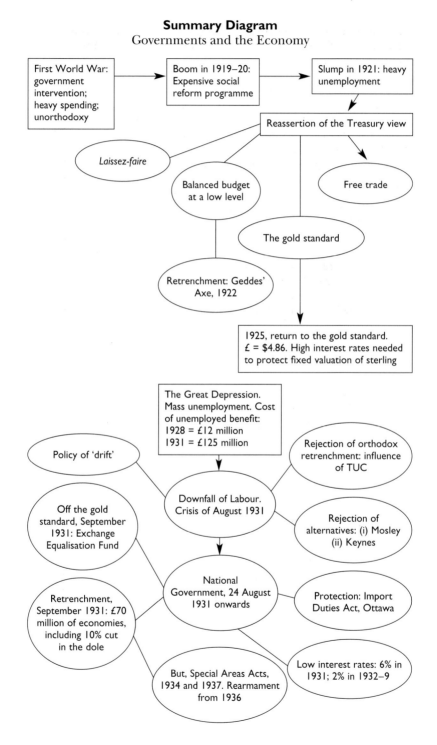

Working on Chapter 6

The headings and sub-headings given in the chapter should help you to organise your notes. Pay particular attention to (i) the return to the gold standard in 1925 and (ii) the depression of 1929–32. In your concluding section, you should reach *your* own conclusion: do not be afraid to disagree with the cautious views the author has presented.

This chapter deals not just with events but also with economic theory. The important thing is to grasp the essential mechanisms involved in both the orthodox Treasury view and in the Keynesian alternative. You might experiment with different ways of noting the main principles in each. Might a diagram help more than straightforward prose? You should also ensure you understand the simple economic processes involved. Do you understand, for instance, the major economic effects of variations in the level of interest rates – on price and employment levels? If you are confident of the theory, your notes can be much briefer than if you are less sure.

Answering essay questions on Chapter 6

This is a popular topic with examiners. Sometimes questions can encompass the whole of the interwar period. Consider the following titles:

1. Explain why politicians failed to solve the problem of unemployment between the wars.
2. With what success did successive governments tackle Britain's economic problems between the two World Wars?

Try writing a brief concluding paragraph for these, bringing out as clearly as you can the differences of approach that each necessitates. Remember that these questions relate not just to government policy but to British economic performance: you will need to be familiar with Chapter 4 as well as this one.

Other titles are narrower and more specific:

3. To what extent was the return to the gold standard in 1925 a major cause of the depression of the 1930s?
4. Did the national governments of the 1930s deal with economic problems more effectively than their Labour predecessors?
5. 'Economic recovery in the 1930s owed little to the actions of governments.' Discuss.
6. How well did the National Government deal with the economic crisis of 1931?

Source-based questions on Chapter 6

1. Keynes and Low on the Treasury

Read the extract on page 122 and study the cartoon on page 126. Answer the following questions:

a) Explain why workers in the 'export industries' (line 1) would be asked to accept wage cuts before workers in other industries. (*2 marks*)

b) Explain what you consider the overall message of the cartoon to be. (*4 marks*)

c) Comment on the depiction of Churchill's crew of the lifeboat. What point was Low attempting to make by drawing them as he did? (*4 marks*)

d) Use your knowledge to explain how valid you consider the criticisms of Keynes and Low to be. (*8 marks*)

7 Conclusion

POINTS TO CONSIDER

Historians spend much of their time pursuing detailed studies, sometimes 'examining the frontiers of knowledge with a microscope'. Such activity is vital, for without original research history would become merely a re-telling of familiar tales with no infusion of new evidence. Nevertheless it is also necessary for historians to raise their eyes from matters of detail in order to consider broader issues. There are times when we should substitute the telescope for the microscope. In this book we have examined Britain's economic performance, industrial relations and society over four decades. What conclusions can be reached about the period as a whole?

1 The Economy

> **KEY ISSUE** What are the positive and negative features of British economic performance in 1900–39?

a) Relative Decline

During the last quarter of the nineteenth century Britain lost the enormous economic lead which it had enjoyed over all other countries. By 1914 the USA and Germany (in some industries) had overtaken its manufacturing output. Yet, on the eve of war, Britain still enjoyed a lead over its competitors in certain spheres (such as finance), and per capita it was still a more highly industrialised country than all others apart from the United States. However, by 1939 it had fallen further behind the USA, it had a smaller share of world manufacturing output than Germany, and it had also been overtaken as an economic power by the Soviet Union.

What had gone wrong? Many answers have been given by historians. Perhaps the most persuasive of these is that British industry failed to modernise. In particular the old staple industries, which had spearheaded the country's economic success in the Victorian era, became technologically backward and lost export markets. In many ways businessmen were short-sighted. The staple industries enjoyed a boom immediately after the First World War, and many industrialists believed that the best days were still ahead for British coal, iron and steel, textiles, and shipbuilding. It took a long time for them to be convinced otherwise.

Britain's relative decline is a fascinating theme, but it has probably attracted too much of the attention of historians studying the years

1900 to 1939. There were also successes in this period, including the growth of new consumer goods industries and improved productivity, and these should not be ignored. Britain's share of world manufacturing output fell over the period as a whole, but it increased between 1928 and 1938, and by this latter date the country was no longer declining *vis-à-vis* its rivals. The fact that larger states with more abundant raw materials were producing more than Britain was hardly an indictment of the British economy: instead, it was perfectly natural. Only the USSR had overtaken Britain's industrial production between the wars, and then only at the tremendous human cost involved in Stalin's five-year plans. Living standards were certainly far higher in Britain than in Soviet Russia. British growth rates may seem unspectacular when compared with those achieved in Stalin's Russia or Hitler's Germany, but then Britain was a democracy while they were dictatorships, and the price to be paid for democracy – which allows individuals to make free economic as well as political choices – is often some degree of economic inefficiency.

Some measure of relative decline was inevitable after the enormous but 'unnatural' lead established in the middle of the previous century. 1880–99 saw this trend established. 1900–39 saw a further relative decline – although the economy continued to grow – but it was hardly a catastrophic one, and it was greater in the 1920s than in the 1930s. Only in the 1950s and 1960s – when, paradoxically, affluence for the bulk of the British public reached hitherto unprecedented levels – did relative decline accelerate alarmingly, and the reasons for this must be sought in the period after 1940 not before.

b) Unemployment

Undoubtedly there was economic success as well as failure between 1900 and 1939, and even during a period of relative decline there were increases in the standard of living. The real shortcoming was Britain's poor record in the realm of unemployment. Cyclical levels were bad, with high unemployment in 1921 and 1930–2, but such problems were short-lived, and most of the unemployed were only out of a job for a few months. Structural unemployment, however, resulted in over one million people being continuously out of work.

A defence can be made of the period after the First World War. Statistics make the problem seem worse than it was. The available figures suggest that in the best years of the interwar period unemployment rates were higher than in the worst years of the late nineteenth and early twentieth centuries. However, before 1921 we only have totals of trade union members out of work, whereas from 1921 onwards we have the much more representative totals of insured workers who were unemployed. Almost certainly, therefore, more workers were unemployed before 1921 than we are aware of. The number out of work should also be assessed in the light of the changing age-structure of Britain's population. While in 1911 64 per cent of the population were aged 15–64, this figure had risen to 70 per cent by 1939. The potential labour force over this period grew by about two million. Yet by the end of the 1930s more people than ever before in Britain's history had found work. Furthermore, the new jobs that were being created tended to be in the highly productive and cap-ital-intensive 'new industries', so that in fact the very success of British industry – in becoming mechanised rather than relying on large num-bers of workers – was tending to limit employment opportunities.

Nevertheless, even when all these factors are taken into account, it must be admitted that Britain's employment record was poor. Mass unemployment existed not only during recessions and depressions, when almost every country suffered from similarly high totals, but during periods of economic buoyancy, when Britain's rivals approached full employment. It took the Second World War to bring new economic life to the 'depressed areas'.

In many ways the economic picture of 1900–39 is a black and white one of sharply contrasting features: affluence and poverty, boom and bust, growth and decay. Yet all too often polemical writers have por-trayed it in terms of black *or* white.

c) Government Involvement

Government economic policies varied greatly during the period from 1900 to 1939. *Laissez-faire* gave way to full-scale mobilisation of the country's economic resources during the First World War, and in 1918–20 it seemed that the government would continue an active, interventionist role. The year 1921, when boom gave way to bust, was therefore a turning point of major significance, allowing traditional ideas to reassert themselves. Politicians attempted to 'return to nor-malcy' – when arguably they should have been forging new policies relevant to Britain's new economic position – culminating in the return to the gold standard in 1925. Yet government activity could not return to pre-war levels. Partly this was due to the longer-term effects of the war, partly to the fact that in an age of universal suffrage poli-ticians had to be responsive to the wishes of the electorate. (Cynics – or perhaps realists – would say that they had to 'buy votes' to stay in power.) The standard rate of income tax, which had been 6 per cent in 1910–14, averaged about 25 per cent in 1918–39, making revenue available for new social services.

Throughout the inter-war period a debate took place on the degree to which governments should seek to influence economic trends. Keynes was the foremost proponent of active intervention. Casting scorn on unimaginative Treasury 'thrift', he believed that unemployment could be significantly reduced by public works and other methods. Government ministers and Treasury officials were influenced but not converted by his thinking. Perhaps a golden opportunity was missed. Politicians before 1939 tended to favour traditional, conservative economic policies. They quite openly preferred to tolerate high levels of unemployment in order to minimise the risks of financial and economic collapse. They simply hoped that one day market forces would provide extra employment opportunities.

'There is little governments can do ... ' insisted the fatalistic Stanley Baldwin. In fact he and other politicians were forgetting the lessons of 1914–18, when governments had done a great deal. During the Second World War, the Treasury turned to radical, Keynesian economic policies, and in 1944, the government felt confident enough of its powers to promise to maintain a 'high and stable level' of employment after the war. If only such confidence had existed earlier, perhaps the mass unemployment of the 1920s and 1930s could have been avoided. State-sponsored modernisation of the economy (as favoured by Keynes, Lloyd George and Oswald Mosley) might have produced far greater economic progress than was in fact achieved.

In defence of governments, it should be said that the Second World War, like the First, created a wholly new psychological climate. In 1940 Britain was fighting for its life, and it was the new political agenda ('victory at all costs ... for without victory there is no survival') which prescribed new economic strategies. It must also be recognised that the promise in 1944 to maintain full employment, though successful for 20 years, now looks like a sick joke. We now know much more about economics and finance than was known in 1900–39 (or at least we think we do), but those who make bold assertions about past mistakes are apt to be discomfited when unexpected twists in present-day economic fortunes shed new light on past issues. Fools are likely to rush in where cautious historians fear to tread! Above all, we must always remember that the people making the decisions at the time did not have the benefit of the historian's hindsight. Developments which are now in the past for us were for them in the future – and this makes a big difference! This is not to say that viable opportunities were not missed in 1900–39 or that politicians should not be criticised: it is simply to urge that we should make an attempt to see issues from the perspectives of the policy-makers themselves.

Another possible missed opportunity was Britain's failure to develop the potentially rich resources of its empire. Politicians in Whitehall had little control over the self-governing Dominions (like Canada and Australia). But there were many dependent colonies whose economies Britain could control. In the 1890s Joseph Chamberlain had referred to 'our undeveloped estate', and by 1939 very little had been done to produce economic growth. The ideal colony, from Whitehall's point of view, was simply one that balanced its budget and so did not require grants-in-aid from Britain. Whether it was rich or poor, developing or stagnant, was of entirely secondary consideration. 'Our crime isn't exploitation,' said Ernest Bevin about the colonial empire; 'It's neglect.' There were climatic and other constraints against economic development; but since no real attempts were made in 1900–39 to foster the economic development of the colonies – certainly not by the Colonial Development Act of 1929, with its miserly funding level of one million pounds a year – it is impossible to prove whether or not an important opportunity was missed.

2 Industrial Relations

KEY ISSUE What fundamental changes occurred from 1900 to 1939?

a) Legislation

Between 1900 and 1939 the legal position of trade unions was greatly clarified. By 1913 it was accepted that unions could use 'peaceful picketing' during strikes (though what this meant in practice was still open to some dispute); they could not be prosecuted for losses incurred by employers during strikes; and they could impose the 'political levy'. However, the rules governing payment of the levy were changed by the Trade Disputes Act of 1927. Henceforth 'contracting in' for those who wanted to pay replaced 'contracting out' for those who did not. This Act was a victory for right-wingers in Britain, but in contrast with developments in Nazi Germany and elsewhere in fascist Europe – where strikes were banned and free trade unions forbidden – it was a small enough defeat for the unions. The 1927 law also ensured that there would be further legislation: the Labour Party promised to repeal the Act when next it formed a majority government. It did so in 1946.

b) The Growth of Trade Unions

Membership of trade unions fluctuated broadly in line with levels of employment and economic prosperity. Membership peaked in 1921, at 8,350,000, just as the economic boom was coming to an end. It did not reach that level again until 1947. Defeat in the General Strike in 1926 lowered the prestige of trade unionism, while the depression of 1929–32 further weakened the movement. Membership sank to 4,400,000 in 1934. But then there was a recovery, so that by 1939 there were more than three times as many union members as in 1900. By the end of our period, therefore, trade unions had become an accepted feature of Britain's economic landscape, recognised by the great majority of the country's employers, who negotiated with them to determine rates of pay.

Although many people tend to remember the spectacular union defeats of 1900–39, the truth of the matter is that only the most optimistic union leaders of 1900 could have hoped to achieve the level of support and authority that the trade union movement had established by 1939.

1914–18 saw the peak of the unions' influence with government, but they were politically influential at other times too, especially in 1931 and again in 1936–9. Having founded the Labour Representation Committee in 1900 – so that, in Bevin's words, the Labour Party 'sprang from the bowels' of the trade union movement – the unions were from 1935 taking a key role in guiding the Party. During the Second World War the unions were to be more influential with government than ever before. In 1940 Bevin became Minister of Labour and began a ten-year alliance with the Labour leader Clement Attlee, which turned out to be undoubtedly the most constructive political partnership in modern British history.

c) Victory for the Moderates

1900–39 saw a victory for 'moderate' trade unionism. Syndicalists and other radicals, seeking to overthrow capitalism and establish workers' control of industry, had been defeated. They had come nearest to success when strikes gripped industry in 1911–12 and 1920–21. For a time during the First World War it seemed that they might exert greater influence on rank and file members than the official union leaders, and they might have become more influential had the General Strike lasted longer. But probably their influence has been exaggerated by left-wing writers sympathetic to their cause, and certainly by 1935 the moderate, 'collaborationist' leaders like Bevin and Citrine effectively dominated the trade union movement. By then trade unions were reformist rather than revolutionary: indeed, instead of providing an alternative to the capitalist economy, they had become an important element in capitalism. Marx had predicted that greedy capitalists would exploit their workers more and more until they rose up in a bloody revolution, but effective trade unionism (among other factors) ensured that workers had far more to lose than simply their chains.

The syndicalists may well have prevented the achievement of greater harmony in industrial relations, for notions of worker control and even worker participation in management decisions were damned by association with them. Instead the unions remained sharply divided from management, perpetuating the 'us' and 'them' attitude which has bedevilled industrial relations in Britain. Opportunities were missed before 1939 to break down this divide. The 'triangular collaboration' of 1914–18 (between government, businessmen and unions) led nowhere, the joint industrial councils of the same period soon ceased to function, and the Mond–Turner talks had few positive consequences. These were significant failures. The nationalised sectors of the economy (like the Central Electricity Board and the British Broadcasting Corporation) were run by boards of directors, just like private companies. After the Second World War, when Attlee's Labour governments of 1945–51 nationalised about 20 per cent of industry (including the mines, thus belatedly fulfilling the recommendations of the 1919 Sankey Commission), the same form of nationalisation was favoured, without any form of worker participation in management. The precedents of the interwar years had been followed. Arguably an important opportunity had been missed to generate better industrial relations by destroying the sharp division between 'employers' and 'employees'.

British industry was, in varying degrees, strike-prone in 1900–39. The stoppages of these years contributed to Britain's relatively poor economic performance. Certainly the loss of 162 million working days during 1926, the year of the General Strike, must have prevented the full force of the worldwide upturn in the trade cycle affecting Britain. Nevertheless, unions and employers managed in the end to establish some sort of *modus vivendi*. This system of industrial relations was in many ways muddled, inefficient and unsatisfactory. Class antagonism was a potent force between the wars, though 'class war' (a term employed by many historians of the period) seems an exaggeration, certainly after 1926. Nevertheless, there was a positive side to this picture as well. The right to withdraw one's labour was an action which some felt was being exercised all too often in Britain, but it was also a precious freedom all too rare in Europe in the 1920s and especially in the 1930s. Strikes were a sign that the British enjoyed a political freedom that was signally lacking in several other European countries.

From 1940 to 1945 Britain's economy and industrial relations system were to be challenged as never before in their history, and by a supposedly ultra-efficient totalitarian regime, in which the government controlled the economy and industrial relations. The fact that Britain was able to mobilise a higher percentage of its economic resources for war than Nazi Germany and at key times to 'out-produce' its enemy, and to do so by more democratic and voluntary means, does not reflect badly on the 1900–39 period.

3 British Society

> **KEY ISSUES** How great, and how beneficial, were social changes over this period?

Fundamental changes in the economy helped to produce fundamental changes in British society, as large numbers of people took jobs in the 'new' industries, as well as in the service sectors of the economy.

In addition, younger elements migrated from the depressed to the more affluent areas. Economic growth meant a higher standard of living for most people: real wages increased and hours of work decreased. There was greater 'disposable income', especially as married couples opted for fewer children. People lived significantly longer, infant mortality declined, and there were new opportunities for the mass of people to enjoy their leisure. It has often been said that British people were more cultured in 1940 than in 1900. They read more books, listened to more music and were far better informed about the world. They were also more entertained, especially by the cinema.

There was also an improved position for women in British society. Not only did women achieve the vote (in 1918 and 1928), but the 'sexual double standard' declined to some degree, as women were able to obtain divorce on the same terms as men. After the death tolls of 1914–18, women constituted a higher proportion of the population and more worked than ever before. On the other hand, women still did not earn the same wages as men, and many lost their jobs after the First World War. There was a renewed campaign to convince women, especially married women, that their place was in the home. But aspirations for greater equality could not be extinguished, and the strides made during the Second World War and since inevitably made the interwar years seem a disappointing time.

There were also better social services in 1939 than in 1900, as the central government assumed greater responsibility for welfare. A significant period of expansion came about under Asquith before 1914. War then stimulated further changes. There was a retreat after the war, but even so there was no return to pre-1914 levels of intervention. Generally, intervention was constructive, not only in providing benefits for the old, sick and unemployed but in care for the young.

However inadequate the system of 1939 seemed to later generations, British social services were perhaps the most advanced in the world. Certainly depression and unemployment in 1929–1933 had far more harmful social consequences in the USA and Germany than in Britain. In the field of education, there were undoubtedly advances, and the British people became more literate than ever before. After the First World War the school leaving age was raised from 11 to 14. Yet the contrast between the education of the poor and of the rich was startling. Few working-class children were able to continue in education after the age of 14, and only 1 per cent of school-leavers had any paper qualifications.

Britain was undoubtedly a class-based society. Incomes were slightly more equal as the 1900–39 period proceeded, but there were vast disparities of wealth. Just as unemployment blighted the economic record of this period, so poverty marred Britain's society.

Poverty had been most commonly caused by low wages before 1914; after 1918 unemployment was its major cause. As a result, there existed in one of the richest countries in the world what one historian has called 'a submerged, slum-dwelling, under privileged, ignorant and undernourished minority'. In this period between 15 and 30 per cent of the population lived in poverty or near to it. We should not underestimate the human tragedy this represented. Nevertheless, it is a fact that the poor in 1900–39 were less poor than in the previous century. Some have computed that a man on the dole in 1939 was better off, in real terms, that a fully employed labourer in 1900. This conclusion goes against the views of many people at the time. J.B. Priestley, for instance, noted in his autobiography in 1939:

> I am not myself conservative-minded and have no respect for the past, yet I do not hesitate to declare that the England of 1914 was superior, in every important development of national life, to the England of to-day.

George Orwell had similar views. He described seeing a typical British crowd in Trafalgar Square in 1936:

> 1 It was impossible, looking about one then, not to be struck by the physical degeneracy of modern England ... What a set they looked! Puny limbs, sickly faces ... Hardy a well-built man or a decent-looking woman, and not a fresh complexion anywhere ... Where are the mon-
> 5 strous men with chests like barrels and monstrous moustaches like the wings of eagles who strode across my childhood's gaze twenty or thirty years ago? Buried, I suppose, in the Flanders mud.

We should be very wary of accepting such impressionistic views. Rowntree certainly found that there had been improvement in York in 1936, compared with 1899 (see page 74); and John Boyd Orr, though highly critical of national nutritional standards in 1936, nevertheless insisted that

> Bad as the picture is ... it is better than the picture of pre-war days. Since then the national dietary has improved ... Accompanying that improvement in diet, there has been a corresponding improvement in national health.

Significantly, whereas 40 per cent of recruits in the Boer war had been declared unfit for military service, there were improvements thereafter. In 1917–18 only one-third were judged 'perfectly fit and healthy', whereas in 1939–45 70 per cent were in this category – a figure that gave no room for complacency but which nevertheless represented a significant betterment.

Another positive feature in the period is British unity when war began in 1939. War of course often produces an upsurge of national identity; but even before the war, British society, despite inequalities, was effectively bound together – by the ties of history, culture and administration, by the media (which now included the BBC as well as newspapers), by sport, the Empire and the monarchy. George V made his first Christmas broadcast in 1932: it was a tremendous success, and thereafter became an annual event. His Silver Jubilee in 1935 produced tremendous national celebrations, and not even the Abdication of Edward VIII the following year harmed the royal sentiment than transcended class differences.

George Orwell, as we have seen (on page 71) believed that Britain was 'most class-ridden country under the sun' (not that he knew much about most of the world's countries). But even he decided in 1940 that Britain constituted 'a family', albeit one 'with the wrong members in control'. Orwell has been called 'the wintry conscience of his generation', and he was acutely aware of what was wrong with British society. Yet even such a pessimist had to admit that 'our age has not been altogether a bad one to live in'.

Working on Chapter 7

You will not need to make detailed notes on this chapter, since it only provides a small amount of new factual information. Instead, you need to engage with the basic issues. History is hard work – you have to formulate your own judgements on the basis of the evidence at your disposal rather than tamely accept what other people think. Try to draw comparisons between Britain in 1900–39 with Britain in earlier and later periods, and with other countries. The problem with this, of course, is that it requires so much knowledge of these other areas – but then the quest for historical understanding is a never-ending one!

Further Reading

There are many general textbooks on the period. **Robert Pearce**, *Britain: Domestic Politics 1918–39* (Hodder & Stoughton, 2nd edition, 2000) is a companion volume to this one. Those who wish to delve deeper should consult the relevant chapters in **Peter Clarke**, *Hope and Glory: Britain 1900–1990* (Allen Lane, 1996) and **Peter Dewey**, *War and Progress: Britain 1914–1945* (Longman, 1997).

1 British Society

The best single volume is undoubtedly **John Stevenson**, *British Society 1914–45* (Penguin, 1984), which is readable and wide-ranging. **John Stevenson** and **Chris Cook**, *The Slump* (Cape, 1977) is also excellent. Those seeking a shorter introduction cannot do better than consult **Stephen Constantine**'s Lancaster pamphlet, *Social Conditions in Britain, 1918–1945* (Methuen, 1983). A volume in the Longman Seminar series, **Rex Pope**, *War and Society in Britain 1899–1948* (Longman, 1991), considers the impact of war, as does **Jocelyn Hunt** and **Sheila Watson**, *Britain and the Two World Wars* (Cambridge University Press, 1990). **Stephen Constantine** et al (eds), *The First World War in British History* (Edward Arnold, 1995) contains some detailed articles on this theme. **Keith Laybourn**, *Britain on the Breadline* (Sutton, 1990) is another valuable work. For developments in social policy, see **Pat Thane**, *The Foundations of the Welfare State* (Longman, 1982).

2 Economic History

Stephen Constantine, *Unemployment in Britain between the Wars* (Longman, 1980) gives a stimulating introduction to one aspect of Britain's inter-war economy. More specialised works on the economy include **Sidney Pollard**, *The Development of the British Economy, 1914–1990* (Edward Arnold, 1992) – a 500-page textbook by one of the experts – and **H.W. Richardson**, *Economic Recovery in Britain 1932–39* (Weidenfeld, 1967) – a controversial study which stresses the positive aspects of Britain's performance in the 1930s. In contrast, **B.W.E. Alford**, *Depression and Recovery? British Economic Growth 1918–39* (Macmillan, 1972) looks more sceptically at the problems of the interwar years. **Malcolm Smith**, *Democracy in a Depression: Britain in the 1920s and 1930s* (University of Wales Press, 1998) is a highly competent account. **David Egerton**, *Science, Technology and the British Industrial 'Decline'* (Cambridge UP, 1996) is short and stimulating.

On the debate on Keynes and the 'Treasury view', two books are well worth consulting: **Robert Skidelsky**, *Politicians and the Slump* (Penguin, 1970) and **Peter Clarke**, *The Keynesian Revolution in the*

Making (Oxford University Press, 1988). A comparison between them is instructive. Skidelsky was writing at a time when it was widely believed that Keynes had 'solved' the problem of unemployment, while Clarke, writing so much later, is far less convinced of this and therefore far less critical of politicians.

3 Volumes on Industrial Relations

An up-to-date but very short account is **John Lovell**, *British Trade Unions, 1875–1933* (Macmillan, 1977). Far more detailed (600 pages compared to 75) is **H.A. Clegg**, *A History of British Trade Unions since 1889, vol. 2 1911–33* (Clarendon Press, 1985). **Alan Fox**, *History and Heritage: the social origins of the British industrial relations system* (Allen and Unwin, 1985) is another large-scale survey.

There are many studies of the General Strike. Perhaps the most useful is **Keith Laybourn**, *The General Strike, Day by Day* (Sutton, 1996). More detailed is **Margaret Morris**, *The General Strike* (Penguin, 1976). **R.A. Florey**, *The General Strike of 1926* (Calder, 1980) covers the same ground but from a definite left-wing point of view.

Two biographies are also worth reading or sampling. **Alan Bullock**, *Life and Times of Ernest Bevin, vol. 1, 1881–1940* (Heinemann, 1960) is a massive work of 650 pages, full of important information, as well as providing a convincing portrait of the most important trade union leader between the wars. **Paul Davies**, *A.J. Cook* (MUP, 1987) is a readable study of one of the key figures in the General Strike.

Sources

Two valuable collections are provided by **Keith Laybourn**, *British Trade Unionism c.1770–1990: A Reader in History* (Sutton, 1991) and *Modern Britain since 1906: A Reader* (I.B. Tauris, 1999). **Asa Briggs**, *They Saw It Happen, 1897–1940* (Blackwell, 1960) has numerous extracts on economic and industrial issues. *The History of the TUC: a pictorial survey of a social revolution* (TUC, 1968) is useful as a lavishly illustrated account. Lastly readers will benefit from consulting the classics of the 1930s, including **George Orwell**, *The Road to Wigan Pier* (Gollancz, 1937); **J.B. Priestley**, *English Journey* (Heinemann, 1934); and **Walter Greenwood**, *Love on the Dole* (Cape, 1933).

Index